7102935016

KU-546-824

THE
UNIVERSAL DECIMAL
CLASSIFICATION

THE
UNIVERSAL DECIMAL
CLASSIFICATION

The history, present status
and future prospects of
a large general classification scheme

by

A C FOSKETT
MA FLA

CLIVE BINGLEY LONDON

FIRST PUBLISHED 1973 BY CLIVE BINGLEY LTD
16 PEMBRIDGE ROAD LONDON WII
SET IN 10 ON 12 POINT LINOTYPE PLANTIN
AND PRINTED IN THE UK BY THE CENTRAL PRESS (ABERDEEN) LTD
COPYRIGHT © A C FOSKETT 1973
0 85157 159 X

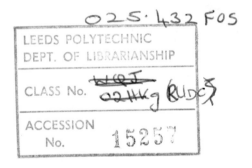

CONTENTS

ILLUSTRATIONS

INTRODUCTION

This study represents the result of some fifteen years of contact with the Universal Decimal Classification, as a user, as a reviser and as a classification teacher. As an Information Officer at the Atomic Energy Research Establishment, Harwell, I was concerned with the use of the Universal Decimal Classification (UDC), both as classifier and as user of the resulting catalogues; I was also directly concerned as Liaison Officer for the Atomic Energy Research Establishment on the United Kingdom Atomic Energy Authority committee for UDC with the development of the Code of Practice which later became the basis of the Special subject edition for nuclear science and engineering. With colleagues, I was responsible for compiling a schedule for Particle accelerators; this work was carried out along the general lines indicated in this study, and is now part of UDC, which indicates that modern ideas can be accommodated within the scheme without undue strain.

Since 1961 I have been involved in teaching the use of UDC to library school students in the United Kingdom and the United States. I have also been a member of the British National Committee for UDC, British Standards Institution Committee BS/OC/20/4, since 1965. Despite the many adverse criticisms which have been made of UDC in recent years, I am convinced that it does indeed have a future if the necessary effort can be made to give the scheme the strong central backing it now lacks, and present users can be persuaded to accept the necessary degree of revision. New methods of publication and revision, utilizing computer techniques, could bring about a radical change in the attitude of many people now antagonistic to UDC. The world wide goodwill that *does* exist must be fostered, but it must also be turned into practical aid in the form of finance for these new ventures.

This study was prepared as a thesis, which has been accepted by the Faculty of Arts of the Queen's University of Belfast for the degree of MA in Library Studies. Because of the current interest in the future

7

of UDC, it was thought that a wider audience would find it of value in stimulating discussion and perhaps even action. Much of the discussion is quite general, and applies to other classification schemes as well as to UDC; it is hoped that students may find it of some use in trying to clarify their ideas about the role of large general classification schemes in the libraries of the future.

Acknowledgements are due to the many people who have influenced my thinking over the years. These include (in alphabetical order): T W Caless, with whom I worked as a consultant; R Freeman, responsible for one of the most significant research projects on UDC; G A Lloyd, Head of the FID Classification Department; D Newcombe, secretary of BS/OC/20/4 and Editor of the English edition; J E Terry of the Atomic Energy Research Establishment, Harwell; J E Wright, Chairman of the British National Committee; and many others. Not least among these is my supervisor, Mr A Maltby, who in the course of several long discussions has greatly helped to clarify the ideas presented here. My wife has, as usual, ensured that family commitments did not distract me too much by shouldering them all herself; without her help, this work would never have been written. I am also grateful to the Governors of the College of Librarianship Wales for their support over the three years that I have worked on my thesis.

December 1972   A C FOSKETT

ABBREVIATIONS AND ACRONYMS

A great many subjects are bespattered with acronyms and similar abbreviations, and Library science is no exception. In many cases the acronym becomes the name, as in Aslib [formerly the Association of Special Libraries and Information Bureaux] and Unesco; in others the shortened form is the only one ever used, so that to use the full version is pedantic. The following list includes all of those used in the text.

AERE	Atomic Energy Research Establishment, Harwell
AIP	American Institute of Physics
AUDACIOUS	AUtomatic Direct ACcess to Information with the On-line Udc System
BLS	British Library Service
BNB	British National Bibliography
BS	British Standard
BSI000	The full English edition of UDC
BSI000A	The abridged English edition of UDC
BSI	British Standards Institution
BTI	British Technology Index
CC	Colon Classification [CC7 seventh edition]
CCC	Central Classification Committee of FID
CFSS	Combined File Search System
COM	Computer Output Microfilm
COSATI	Committee on Scientific and Technical Information [Part of the US President's Federal Council on Science and Technology]
CRG	Classification Research Group
DC	Decimal Classification (Dewey) [DC16 sixteenth edition]
E & C	Extensions and Corrections to the UDC
EJC	Engineers Joint Council
ERIC	Educational Resources Information Center
EURATOM	European Atomic Energy Commission

FID	International Federation for Documentation
FID/CCC	Central Classification Committee of the FID
IAEA	International Atomic Energy Agency
ICSU	International Council of Scientific Unions
IIB	Institut International de Bibliographie
IID	Institut International de Documentation
INIS	International Nuclear Information Service
LC	Library of Congress classification
MARC	MAchine Readable Cataloguing
MEDLARS	MEDical Literature Analysis and Retrieval System
MeSH	Medical Subject Headings
NSA	Nuclear Science Abstracts
NT(A)	Narrower Term (Additional) [used in Thesaurofacet]
OSTI	Office for Scientific and Technical Information
P-Note	Proposal for amendment to UDC schedules
PMEST	Personality, Matter, Energy, Space, Time [fundamental categories postulated by Ranganathan for subject analysis]
PRECIS	PREserved Context Indexing System
RT	Related Term [used in thesauri]
SDI	Selective Dissemination of Information
SRC	Standard Reference Code
	Standard Roof Classification
TEST	Thesaurus of Engineering and Scientific Terms (EJC)
UDC	Universal Decimal Classification
UF	Use For [used in thesauri]
UKAEA	United Kingdom Atomic Energy Authority
UNISIST	World science information system: feasibility study and recommended future programme
USAEC	United States Atomic Energy Commission

CHAPTER 1

PRESENT AND FUTURE NEEDS FOR A GENERAL
CLASSIFICATION SCHEME

The first detailed general classification scheme for libraries in the sense that the words are now used was that devised by Melvil Dewey for the library of Amherst College and published (anonymously) in 1876.[1] Dewey's purpose was two-fold: to provide a method of arranging books on library shelves in an order which would be helpful to the users, and to provide a method of arranging surrogates of the books themselves in a catalogue to facilitate the finding of information. Both of these needs still exist, but in recent years the tendency has been to concentrate on the second, for a number of reasons.

While books continue to be an important source of information, their place has been taken in many subject areas by other forms of presentation: periodicals, technical reports, audio-visual materials, for example. These do not lend themselves to display on shelves, and indeed in many cases are not suitable for open access methods at all. This means that the basic reason for classification as a means of shelf arrangement —to present readers with a helpful order of physical objects—does not apply in these areas. There is, however, still an urgent need to be able to find information when it is needed, through catalogues, lists and bibliographies, so the second need still exists; indeed, the fact that information is now presented in smaller units, each of which may deal with a very specific subject, makes the approach through surrogates far more important than it has been in the past.[2]

Most of the large general classification schemes which have been compiled have proved inadequate for the detailed arrangement of, and access to information through, surrogates in the form of card catalogues and printed bibliographies. The Universal Decimal Classification (UDC) is the only one which has been developed with this purpose, rather than shelf arrangement, in mind, and this has in many ways proved insufficient for today's needs. This inadequacy has led to the development of other methods of information retrieval which have appeared to do away with the need for classification.

Alphabetical subject headings have been used by the vast majority of libraries in the United States (following the lead of the Library of Congress), and by many British libraries, in their catalogues; they have also been used in many bibliographies, a notable example being the *British technology index,* which uses a system of subject headings devised in accordance with the theories of E J Coates, the editor.[3] It can be shown that a system of alphabetical headings must rely to some extent on a classified approach if relationships between subjects are to be shown in any systematic fashion, but it does not have to be linked to any particular scheme; BTI uses several schemes, including UDC, but does not rely exclusively on any of them.[4]

A number of special classification schemes have been devised and many of these have proved very satisfactory in use.[5] Because they are restricted to coverage of a limited number of concepts, many of the problems of general schemes which try to cover the whole of knowledge do not arise, and more detail can be included in the area covered. In practice, however, no library or bibliography exists in a vacuum, and it is always found necessary to make provision for ' fringe ' subjects; those topics which are not central to the subject area being covered but which are likely to be represented in any library specializing in the ' core ' area. For example, the classification of library science compiled by members of the Classification Research Group includes in its fringe schedules such topics as printing and bookselling.[6] It is often the case that use is made of a general classification scheme to cater for fringe subjects, as for example in the library of the College of Librarianship Wales, which borrows extensively from the UDC for fringe materials. There is again no compulsion to use an existing scheme; it is perfectly feasible to compile one's own schedules.

A third very significant development in information retrieval has been the introduction of post-coordinate indexing. In this method, subjects represented in documents are broken down into their constituent concepts, which are then used for indexing the document. Concepts may be associated at the moment of search (post-coordinated, *ie* coordinated after storage rather than before, as is usual with conventional classification schemes or alphabetical headings). The method involves the introduction of new physical forms, such as Uniterm cards or 'peek-a-boo', and it is used in many computer based systems, *eg* MEDLARS. As with alphabetical subject headings, there is a need to introduce an element of the systematic approach in order to establish relationships between subjects, but here again there is no need to rely on any particular scheme.[7]

The use of large general classification schemes for shelf arrangement is thus becoming of less significance than in the past, and the use of such schemes in information retrieval systems has been abandoned by perhaps the majority of users. What justification can one see, then, for the continuation of their existence? In particular, what is likely to be the future of UDC? Can it serve any useful purpose in the library world of the future, and if so, does it need to be altered in any way to make it viable? It is the intention of this study to examine the present state of UDC in the light of its past history, and to propose ways in which the future development may be directed so that the scheme may continue to perform a useful function. To do this, it is first necessary to examine the potential functions of a large general classification scheme, and the nature of the kind of scheme which may be of value in the future.

CONTINUING NEED FOR GENERAL CLASSIFICATION SCHEMES

It has been pointed out that special classifications often rely on a general classification for fringe areas. The Classification Research Group developed in its first decade techniques which were adequate for the compilation of special schemes, but were gradually forced to the conclusion that a general scheme was necessary if time was not to be wasted in compiling fringe schedules independently each time a new special classification was needed. In recent years the CRG have devoted most of their efforts to this end, and their proposals will be examined to try to establish whether they can be applied to UDC.[8]

A classification scheme, in which the order of subjects is maintained by means of a notation, is not linked to any particular language. There are editions of UDC in some fifteen languages already, and there is no reason why there should not be further editions. On the other hand, alphabetical systems are linked to the language in which they are developed. It seems possible that a classification scheme could serve as a device for linking alphabetical headings in different languages, particularly as classification schemes are based on concept analysis rather than just words. Post-coordinate systems rely on words, and in consequence even such a broadly based system as MEDLARS is of very limited value outside the English-speaking world, whereas a system based on UDC could be used everywhere irrespective of language.

Last but by no means least, it is important to remember that UDC and similar schemes are familiar to a great many people, and there are many millions of documents classified by them. By developing them in such a way that they can be used in libraries of the future, it is possible to avoid abandoning the libraries of the past. However, it is equally important to realize that the trend away from classification schemes reflects a dissatisfaction with their functioning which cannot be allowed to continue; the revised schemes must be adequate for the libraries of the future, not merely for those of the past or present.

THE NEED FOR STRUCTURAL CHANGES

It seems likely that any general classification scheme of the future will differ in at least two respects from most of today's schemes. The first of these major changes will be an abandonment of orientation towards disciplines. All the general schemes used at all widely at present are discipline oriented: that is to say, their major division of knowledge is into conventional disciplines such as Physics, Biology, Engineering or Music. It is very difficult to incorporate the kind of cross-disciplinary development which is becoming more and more common nowadays as research breaks down barriers between disciplines. Should Biophysics be accounted a branch of Physics or of Biology? Is Electronic Music to be placed with Music or Electronic Engineering? There is no satisfactory answer to such questions if the main structure of the scheme in use is tied to an essentially obsolescent approach. (Disciplines arise rather slowly as the results of research are incorporated into standard teaching; by this time, research will already be undermining the basis on which they are constructed.) Only one major scheme has made any attempt so far to depart from this approach: the Subject Classification of J D Brown.[9] In this, analysis is centred on concretes, with disciplines as subsidiary concepts. Unfortunately, Brown's scheme was unsatisfactory in many respects and in consequence was never successful on any large scale; his ideas on subject analysis tended to be discarded *in toto,* and have only recently been restored to their true significance. The work of CRG has been concentrated on the construction of a non-discipline oriented scheme, which will be described later. Schemes such as UDC have had difficulties in incorporating new topics such as molecular biology and cybernetics, and attempts to restructure the scheme in order that it should reflect more accurately the present set of disciplines have met with considerable opposition from users, who have a vested interest in the continuation of the *status quo*.

The other respect in which future schemes will differ significantly from those of the past is that of synthesis. In his first edition, Dewey enumerated all the subjects he thought would be needed; so that one finds, for example, topics such as English grammar, French grammar, German grammar, listed in the schedules. As the scheme was relatively small (less than 1,000 topics listed altogether) 'minor' languages did *not* have an enumerated subdivision for grammar and it was therefore not possible to specify such subjects precisely. Dewey did, however, recognize at the early stage that one might wish to specify certain aspects of a subject at almost any point; for example, one might wish to indicate that a document dealt with the subjects in a particular place (the British steel industry, French schools, American men of science). It is obviously impractical to enumerate all of these, and in his second edition Dewey made provision for notational synthesis, that is, the combining of pieces of notation from different parts of the schedules, to allow for composite subjects. Dewey took a rather limited view of the need for synthesis, and it was left to Ranganathan[10] to point out that composite subjects can arise in *any* subject area, and we need therefore to make provision for synthesis at all points. Thus, where Dewey had enumerated English grammar, French grammar and so on, Ranganathan enumerated only languages—English, French . . .—and grammatical 'problems'—grammar, etymology . . .—but provided notation which could be combined to specify the requisite composite subjects.

Other classificationists had seen the need for synthesis, for example H E Bliss in his *Bibliographic classification*,[11] but none of them had applied it as thoroughly as Ranganathan. The CRG, who adopted and expanded many of his principles, have demonstrated the use of notational synthesis in all of the special schemes they have compiled, and have examined many of the problems involved. UDC began as a mixture between the very largely enumerative scheme of Dewey and the type of synthetic scheme to be developed some forty years later by Ranganathan. Many of the more recent schedules are entirely synthetic, but there remain many which are not, and these create something of a problem.

It must be realized that synthesis of notation is a device to help the classifier, not the user. It enables the classifier to specify composite subjects which may not have been foreseen by the classificationist (*ie* the compiler of the scheme) but which nevertheless arise in documents, while at the same time it enables the schedules to be kept within reasonable limits. The difference may be seen in Belles-Lettres, for which the schedule in the Library of Congress classification,[12] largely but not entirely enumerative, occupies some 2,000 pages, while the schedule in UDC, using synthesis, covers less than a page. But the final result achieved in terms of shelf arrangement or information retrieval could be exactly the same whichever scheme was used. Notational synthesis is now accepted as being essential in any scheme of classification intended to be used by classifiers other than the compiler, and the extent to which satisfactory synthesis is possible in UDC will be a significant factor in determining its future potential. (In the Library of Congress, classifier and classificationist are normally the same person; in these circumstances, the need for synthesis does not arise in the same way.)

Synthesis imposes a number of demands on notation. It must be possible to combine any two or more pieces of notation unambiguously and precisely, and also to be able to locate particular combinations in searching. These demands are not compatible with the extreme simplicity of notation to be found in the *Decimal classification*, which uses only arabic numerals, yet too complex a notation can be disconcerting for both classifier and user. UDC has not solved this problem satisfactorily as yet.

The need for synthesis to give manageable schedules at the same time as power to specify new composite subjects in detail implies an equal need for analysis. If pieces of notation representing single concepts are to be combined to represent composite subjects, the single concepts must first of all be identified. If the composite subjects found in a collection of documents falling into a reasonably homogeneous subject area (*eg* Library science) are analysed, it is found that they fall into a rather limited number of categories, usually called facets, such that the concepts, or foci, which fall into any one facet are mutually exclusive: they cannot be combined in any feasible composite subject. For example, in Philology, English, French, German and other languages fall into a languages facet, while syntax, etymology and other concepts fall into another quite separate facet: a 'problems' or 'energy' facet. It is possible to combine English and syntax, French and etymology; but not English and French, nor syntax and etymology. It is evident that the preliminary analysis must be very detailed if later synthesis is not to be unsatisfactory.[13]

ANOMALIES REVEALED BY ANALYSIS

If this analysis is carried out for a variety of limited subject areas, it soon becomes clear that there are some facets which are valid generally, and not merely within a particular subject. Although grammatical problems are peculiar to Philology, the same is not true of languages, which may appear as an aspect of Belles-Lettres, and which may also characterize one facet of the 'form of presentation', in this case the language in which the work is written. Place and Time are other common facets. There are in addition facets which, although not common to all topics, recur throughout a wide area; one may cite the 'parts' facet in Engineering, or the 'materials' facet in Chemical technology, as examples. Other facets recur in subject areas which may be separated by the discipline-oriented approach: a 'plants' facet will be found in Botany, but also in Agriculture.

The same concept may thus appear in a number of different places in a general classification scheme. This is unsatisfactory, in that it makes both classifying and searching more haphazard. In classifying, one is faced with the problem of determining the discipline into which a concept will fall, while in searching, it is very easy to overlook related material which happens to be filed within another discipline or subject area. Ideally, each concept should be enumerated once and once only, with notation which enables it to be used in any required combination to specify a composite subject. The work of the CRG has been directed towards this end, which becomes of considerable significance if computer searching is contemplated.

THE EFFECTS OF MECHANIZATION

Mechanization is becoming of increasing significance in information retrieval. Computers are already used in the manipulation of index entries in such tools as BTI and MEDLARS, and the MARC Project[14] is likely to lead within a very few years to quite general reliance on centrally generated cataloguing copy in machine-readable form. A good deal of research is in progress with a view to the development of computer techniques for indexing without human intervention. Computers are valuable in that they enable searches to be performed in a reasonable time which would be extremely time-consuming if performed manually, but there is a risk entailed: the reader may be presented with more information than he can use, while still missing some highly relevant material. An information retrieval system should be flexible enough to perform a limited search, yielding a few documents to satisfy the reader with this kind of need, but also to perform a detailed search, revealing all the documents in the collection likely to be of value, for those occasions where this kind of search is necessary, for example in patents collections. The danger in mechanized systems is that unless the preliminary indexing has been very carefully controlled, neither type of search will be carried out satisfactorily, and a high proportion of documents of only marginal interest will be revealed.

A further point is that for mechanization to be satisfactory, it is essential to eliminate inconsistencies in whatever system is used. It is not feasible to write exceptions into the computer program if there are very many of these. For example in the *Decimal Classification* up to edition 16 we find that accounting in special industries or businesses is all dealt with at one place—with a few exceptions including Librarianship. Accounting in Librarianship is found in Librarianship. Now many other anomalies of the same kind occur, and this led the British National Bibliography to change its method of classification at the beginning of 1971; instead of trying to impose consistency on the *Decimal Classification,* BNB now accepts the eighteenth edition as it stands, and instead imposes the consistency on its own alphabetical subject indexing method, PRECIS.[15] UDC has eliminated many of the problems of consistency that we find in Dewey, largely through its degree of synthesis, but there are nevertheless still many inconsistencies left, and these are obviously difficult to cater for in a mechanized system.

Another weakness of UDC revealed by one investigation of its potential in the mechanized system was the lack of precision with which some of the notation is normally used; in particular, the colon is used in a variety of ways which affect considerably its value as a retrieval tool.[16]

THE PROBLEM TO BE DISCUSSED

We have then to consider a number of problems, and to try to reach some conclusions as to likely solutions. What is likely to be the future need for large general classification schemes? Can the UDC be made to meet these needs? Can other ideas developed in recent years point the way forward to a possible solution? The origins of UDC will first be discussed, to elucidate the historical reasons for some of the peculiarities and anomalies that we find in the scheme today; the line of thought which has been pursued in recent years by the Classification Research Group will be examined; and finally an attempt will be made to see whether these ideas could be applied within the framework of UDC to make possible the future development of this particular scheme.

CHAPTER 2

ORIGINS OF THE UNIVERSAL DECIMAL CLASSIFICATION

Melvil Dewey first proposed his *Classification and Subject Index* in 1873, and in the fifteen years following this he produced another three editions. The system also became known on the continent of Europe. Two Belgians, Paul Otlet and Henri LaFontaine, were instrumental in beginning work on an International Bibliography of Social Sciences in 1889; they were particularly interested in Sociology, Law, Statistics and Political Economy, but also in Philology and Literature. They set up the Office Internationale de Bibliographie with the idea of compiling an index to recorded knowledge; their ideas were on the grand scale, and they envisaged an international organization which would make this a practical proposition. It was fairly clear that it would not be possible for one organization to do all the work itself, and they therefore looked round for some means whereby items of interest could be indexed on a world wide basis and fed into a central catalogue. In order to do this it was necessary to have some kind of international language for the subject indexing; Dewey's *Classification* was the first suitable system to have been devised, and they therefore wrote to Dewey asking for his permission to develop the scheme for their own purposes.[17]

NEED TO DEVELOP THE DECIMAL CLASSIFICATION

Dewey had conceived his scheme as being applied to the arrangement of books on shelves. Though he did also suggest its use in catalogues, he was thinking of catalogues of books, where the problems of subject specification would be similar to those of shelf arrangement. Otlet and LaFontaine, on the other hand, were much more interested in periodical articles, news items, and other similar documents, and therefore needed a rather more detailed system. They therefore wrote to Dewey to ask him if he would be agreeable to their developing his scheme for their International Index, and he agreed. By 1895, Otlet and LaFontaine and their fellow workers had classified some 400,000 cards for their ' Universal Index '. They presented this to the world at a conference on International Bibliography held in 1895; their ideas obviously appealed, for within eight days the petition to the king which was the major product of this conference had been accepted, and the Office became an official Belgian organization. Otlet and LaFontaine were obliged to add a great many devices to Dewey's original scheme; these devices would now be described as synthetic, although the term was not used at that time. For example, sample pages in the paper presented by Otlet and LaFontaine to the conference show the use of parentheses to indicate place and thus distinguish it clearly from the notation for subjects; in Dewey it was certainly possible to add notation for place to that for subjects by using the indicator 09, but this was more clumsy and less flexible than the use of parentheses. The new system was particularly developed to show bibliographical forms and dates, since these were added to the class numbers for subjects to specify in many cases the source, *eg* a press cutting or a periodical.

The need to be able to relate subjects appearing in different places in the main schedules had also been noted; the pieces of notation were to be joined together by a colon, to show some kind of relationship, or a plus sign, to show two or more subjects, separated in the scheme, which together formed the subject of the document. In addition to these methods of showing various kinds of relationship, the need for facets within particular subjects had also been seen, though of course the word ' facet ' was not used until Ranganathan introduced it. The idea of methods of division other than genus to species was recognized, and it was suggested that .o should be used to introduce the notation for these subsidiary facets; for example,

591.1   Physiology
597   Fish
597.01   Physiology of Fish

In addition, the need to be able to specify names, languages and bibliographical forms at the same time as subjects was recognized and indeed we find that rules are given for the way in which these various pieces of notation were to be combined:

Subject-specific subject (:)-place-time-form-language.

In addition to the above modifications of Dewey's scheme, which are still used in UDC, we find others which in the course of time have been abandoned. Perhaps the most interesting of these was the significant use of the point, eg 614.88.2; 617.558.2; 617.5582.14; 617.5582.88.3. This particular notational device has been abandoned, and the point is now only used as a pause device, breaking up otherwise uncomfortable blocks of notation into sets of three digits, except when it is followed by a zero, when it does have some meaning still.

It is clear that at this early date Otlet and LaFontaine, though owning their debt to 'la géniale invention de M Melvil Dewey', had already departed in many major ways from his original scheme. Nevertheless, they did adhere to his outline; indeed, it was a condition of the permission to use the scheme that they should not change any numbers, but were at liberty to add to them. In view of the criticism which has arisen in recent years, it is interesting to note that the Royal Society was of the opinion in 1896 that the *Decimal Classification* was inadequate and they proposed an attempt at revision in class 500 Science to give what might be considered today a more satisfactory outline; the first half of the schedule remains the same but we then find:

560	Zoology
570	Botany
580	Physiology
590	Anthropology

instead of the rather unsatisfactory removal of Physiology to 610, as part of Medicine, which we still find in Dewey. The increase in detail given by Otlet and LaFontaine's extensions is shown by the fact that they had some 40,000 headings in the full schedule by 1896, as opposed to 7,418 in the 5th edition of the Decimal Classification, on which their expansion was based.

PUBLICATION OF THE SCHEDULES

Otlet and LaFontaine had in mind the development of an Universal Index, but the work they had carried out in the expansion of Dewey was obviously of interest to other people. Parts of the expanded schedules were published in the *Bulletin of the IIB* (Institut International de Bibliographie), and eventually the whole of the expanded schedules were published in 1905 as the *Manuel du répertoire universel bibliographique,* which drew attention to the original purpose of the expansion but nevertheless made it available to any other interested parties. The 'Brussels Expansion' as it came to be known was in fact adopted quite widely on the continent of Europe and became known in

Britain also, with an important article about it published in the Library Association Record in 1907.[18]

The fact of publication meant that the scheme, although very closely related to the Universal Index, was no longer tied completely to that particular tool. The index in fact suffered a crippling blow with the outbreak of the Great War in 1914, and although it was on the way to a recovery in the early 1920's, it eventually succumbed when it had to be moved from its home to make way for a trade exhibition.[19] By this time, however, the use of the 'Brussels Expansion' had reached the point where it could stand on its own, and in 1927 work began on the second edition, published under the name *Classification Décimale Universelle*. Otlet and LaFontaine were still the major figures, but they were joined by a third, who was destined to play an extremely important part in the development of UDC over the next thirty years: Frits Donker Duyvis. Donker Duyvis had been employed by the Dutch Patent Office, but was seconded to take charge of the revision of the schedules for Science and Technology, to assist Otlet and LaFontaine whose concern was, as we have already seen, mainly with the Social Sciences and Humanities. The second edition, in French as was the first, was completed by 1933 and in the following year work began on the third edition, the German *Dezimal Klassifikation;* this edition was eventually completed in 1952, having been interrupted for some ten years by the second world war.

Donker Duyvis had become secretary of the IIB in 1929, and in 1931 the Institut changed its name to Institut International de Documentation (IID), and in 1937 this was changed again to Fédération International de Documentation (FID): these changes broadened the scope of the organization, but did not in any way detract from the significance of the UDC within it, and as secretary Donker Duyvis was in a very good position to further his prime interest, the development of UDC. In Britain, the scheme found an ardent support in Dr S C Bradford, librarian of the Science Museum Library. Bradford was also struck by the possibility of building up a 'Universal Index', though he did restrict the subject area to Science and Technology; he developed the British version of UDC for this purpose, but his index suffered the same fate as the Brussels index and eventually succumbed from an excess of input in relation to a very limited demand. However, the work done by the Science Library was the foundation for the development of the full English edition, the fourth edition of UDC to be started. Work began on this in 1940 under the auspices of the British Standards Institution, the national body for UDC English editions, and the first schedules were published in 1943.[20] Work on the English edition has been bedevilled by lack of funds and the lack of adequate staff at the BSI until quite recently, and the expected completion date for the full English edition is now the end of 1972. Other full editions have been prepared in Spanish, Japanese, Polish, and Portuguese, but the key edition, the last edition to be completed, has been the German third edition already referred to. This has been partially updated, and revision is still in progress.

THE INFLUENCE OF DONKER DUYVIS

Donker Duyvis originally joined the UDC editorial team in order to take charge of the revision for the second edition of the Science and Technology schedules. He continued as secretary of the organization under its new titles after the retirement of Otlet and LaFontaine, and gradually took over complete responsibility for the revision. The second edition has been revised by a team, but since then basic revision has been carried out in a rather different manner which has been both a strength and a weakness. The details of this revision effort are discussed later; the point at issue here is that for some years the whole responsibility for the revision of UDC was borne by one man, assisted certainly by a great many other people, but basically working on his own. One consequence of this was the extensive development of the schedules for Science and Technology in relation to those of the Social Sciences and Humanities; it has been pointed out that Science and Technology together accounted for something over eighty per cent of the schedules, although in Dewey's original outline they were expected to occupy only one-fifth.[21]

Another point concerns the actual revision mechanism, details of which are given later. Donker Duyvis was not a classification theorist; he was essentially a subject specialist who gained a knowledge of working with this one particular scheme. An important consequence of this was that the instructions which were given to people wishing to revise or expand sections of UDC were very largely concerned with the administrative details; no guidance whatever was given on ' classification ' matters, such as the way the notation should be allocated.[22] This led to all kinds of anomalies, for example in the development of the special auxiliaries. If one goes back to the early days, it is possible to see some distinction being made between auxiliaries introduced by a hyphen, and those introduced by .o; the former were meant to parallel numbers in the main tables, while the latter were always expected to be subsidiary and thus did not appear in the main tables. However, even the briefest study of the schedules shows that this theory was not followed out in practice. Dubuc has listed the places in the schedules where these two auxiliaries are used, and a study of this tabulation shows that there is no consistency in their use at all.[23] Another area in which this lack of central theoretical control is seen is in the ' point of view numbers ', introduced by .oo. These are, if taken on their own, fairly sensible and helpful, but if they are compared with schedules already existing in the main tables or in some of the special auxiliary tables listed at intervals throughout the main schedules, it becomes clear that there is a great deal of overlap between the two. Had Donker Duyvis been more expert in classification, perhaps these anomalies would not have occurred; however, there is no doubt that the amount of work involved in organizing a complex classification scheme of this size, and at the same time bearing in mind the needs for a wide variety of users, is very great indeed, and it is possible that there was simply too much work for one man to achieve it satisfactorily on his own. One should also be wary of blaming Donker Duyvis for not having followed theories of classification which were in their infancy when he was carrying out his work; though the early development of UDC shows in practice quite a large measure of adherence to the ideas now called ' facet analysis ', it was a pragmatic scheme and not one based on theoretical considerations. The latter came in, if they came in at all, as a bonus.

THE REVISION PROCEDURE

The preceding paragraph may be clarified further if we consider the procedure used for revision. The second edition was prepared by a team working together under the direction of Donker Duyvis, Otlet and LaFontaine, but since then revision has been decentralized. Users are themselves responsible for developing new extensions or amending existing schedules, and the mechanism set up to enable them to do this is somewhat clumsy. A user wishing to review a particular section should normally get in touch with his national body: in Britain, the British Standards Institution. They will ascertain whether any revision is in progress elsewhere, and if not, they may well ask the original enquirer to prepare a draft extension himself. This draft is submitted to the national body and considered by a subject panel; once it has the approval of the national subject panel and the national body it will be considered by the International Subject Panel. Difficulties may already have arisen, but it will be appreciated that these are exacerbated if the International Committee has members in Britain, Germany and Japan and possibly one or two other countries as well, as was the case with the panel considering revisions of Nuclear Science and Technology. Once an extension has been approved by the International Subject Committee it is forwarded to the Central Committee, FID/CCC, the Central Classification Committee of the International Federation for Documentation. This committee will consider it in the light of its interaction with other parts of the scheme; does it clash for example with already existing schedules within another subject area? Assuming that it meets with approval, it is published as a P-Note. [Originally there were two kinds of P-Note, PE, Projects d'Extension, and PP, Projects Provisoires. The first of these related to extensions or amendments which had gone through the machinery described above; the second were used for proposals emanating from the Central Classification Committee and thus liable to rather more widespread comment than those already approved by Subject Committees.] Publication in P-Note form makes the proposed extension public, and in effect it lies on the table for four months, during which time any interested party may comment. If no comments are received during this four month period, it is assumed that potential users are satisfied, and the schedule becomes part of the official UDC. If on the other hand objections are received the proposal may well be withdrawn for further consideration.

It will be seen that in the situation in which UDC found itself, under the direction of one individual working almost entirely alone, the degree of control over the revision which could be exercised was perhaps less than would now be regarded as desirable. When we add to this the point that the individual in question was not a classification theorist, then it becomes clear that we should not expect the revision of UDC during that period to conform to any sound theoretical pattern. The remarkable fact is that the UDC did indeed not only continue to exist but thrived under the direction of Donker Duyvis, a tribute to a remarkable man. However, the information explosion after the second world war began to place an intolerable strain on this rather unsatisfactory mechanism. For example, a new schedule for aero space engineering took some ten years to make its way through the mill, by which time one may suspect that it was a little out of date, and had

26

been overtaken by events.[24] A schedule for particle accelerators developed by the present author in collaboration with two colleagues took some two years to become part of the official UDC even though no substantive objections were received at any point in its career.[25]

The slow pace of revision was paralleled by the clumsiness of the publication mechanism. It has been mentioned already that accepted P-Notes became part of the official UDC, but the exact mechanism of this was not entirely satisfactory itself. Accepted P-Notes were gathered together and published every six months in the *Extensions and corrections to the UDC;* these six monthly publications of P-Notes were progressively cumulated into three year volumes, after which a new series was begun. The German edition which formed the base from which progress was made was itself in a rather difficult state; much of the work had been done before the outbreak of war in 1939, but there had been a long delay before the work was finally completed in 1952, and in consequence a supplementary volume, the *Ergänzungen,* had been published to gather together all the changes which had been made while the German edition had been in progress. The user of UDC had therefore to take the German edition, and then check not only the *Ergänzungen* but also five series of *Extensions and corrections* to see him through the period up to the end of 1965. Fortunately, these publications have now all been cumulated themselves into one set of six volumes, but we still have to use the German edition plus the cumulated *Extensions and corrections,* plus the two series of *Extensions and corrections* covering 1966-68 and 1969-71, if we are to be sure that we have the most up to date version of UDC that is available. The position has not been entirely remedied by the publication of the English edition; while it is certainly correct that the recently published schedules do take into account the recent revision, many of the schedules go back a number of years, some indeed to 1943, and these must certainly be modified in the way just described.

Unless we appreciate the situation between 1930 and 1959, when Donker Duyvis retired through ill-health, it is difficult to understand how a scheme of this size and importance could have been developed in such an unsystematic way. However, we should not forget that similar anomalies occurred in the Dewey Decimal Classification right up to the fourteenth edition, published in 1942, despite the fact that Dewey himself supervised the compilation and publication of the first thirteen editions. It is also important to remember that UDC was no longer being used by any one particular central agency, as it had been during the first thirty years of its life. There is no doubt that the existence of a powerful central agency, with a clearly defined policy, can make a tremendous difference to a classification scheme, which must of its very nature be based on literary warrant, *ie* the needs of collections of documents; UDC was indeed developed according to the needs of collections of documents but these collections were many and disparate, and the necessary central unity was lacking.

EXTERNAL CRITICISM

In 1961, Unesco published the results of two surveys of UDC that it had commissioned; the first of these, by B C Vickery, covered the Science and Technology schedules, the second, by Barbara Kyle, covered the Social Sciences.[26] These two reports were hostile, and suggested that UDC could, for a variety of reasons, no longer fulfil its functions as an adequate international general classification scheme. Lack of development in modern subjects, lack of balance between the development of different subject areas, and the adherence to an outdated framework—that of the *Dewey Decimal Classification*—were all cited as reasons for abandoning UDC and looking for some more acceptable substitute. Coming as they did at the same time as Donker Duyvis's retirement and premature death, these criticisms could have been a death blow, but in fact they were not. The Central Classification Committee gave a great deal of thought to ways in which they might react to these basic criticisms. One way was to abandon once and for all the adherence to Dewey's outline which had been an essential part of the scheme originally, had been gradually eroded between the wars, but had been restated after the war as an essential feature of the scheme. In the *Review of documentation* in 1963, a set of articles was published outlining possible reallocations of the notation to give a more realistic framework, and one more in line with current thought.[21] These proposals for a brave new world were welcomed at the time, but made little progress, and have now to some extent been overtaken by events; the present state is discussed in the next chapter. For the moment, let us merely emphasize that these proposals were made, and achieved a measure of acceptance, though not any very great measure of implementation. There was also a change in the Central Secretariat, an important position being taken over by G A Lloyd, previously editor of the English edition, who did have some understanding of current classification theories and techniques, and who has in fact endeavoured to apply these through the years to the development of the scheme. The instructions on how to revise existing UDC schedules were themselves revised, and now give some guidance on how to construct a schedule using facet analysis; it is however suggested later herein that they do not go far enough, and a rather more elaborate proposal for revision methods was put forward in 1969, but appeared not to win favour.[27]

DEVELOPMENT OF ABRIDGED EDITIONS

The first way in which UDC schedules became available in English was through the publication by the Science Museum Library of *Classification for works on Pure and Applied Science in the Science Museum Library* of which the third edition appeared in 1936. This was quite a brief version of the full schedules available at that time, and in 1948 it formed the basis of the first official abridged English edition.[28] This edition was intended so to speak as a stop gap measure to make the schedules at least partially available in English pending the publication of the full translation; however, they gained a great measure of acceptance in their own right, and a second abridged English edition was published in 1957. This was a considerable improvement on the first; the schedules were revised completely to bring them up to date not only in content but in terminology also, and the index was very greatly expanded from about 2,000 to some 20,000 entries. The third English abridged edition was published in 1961, and is the latest available, work on a revision of this having given way to the requirements of producing the full English edition. Abridged editions are also available in some fourteen other languages, and form a major way in which UDC has been made available throughout the world. One should also mention the trilingual abridged edition, which had the French, German and English texts side by side in three columns; this was published in 1958, and a ten year supplement was published in 1968; the latter is in fact the most up to date abridged version available in English, and contains some features developed since the publication of the 1961 edition.[29]

The abridged edition was developed on a rather haphazard basis; at least, that is the impression that one gets on studying its relationship to the full edition. Some of the schedules are very similar indeed; there appears to have been little abbreviation from the full to the abridged edition. Others, on the other hand, seem to have been ' massacred ', with very little of the full schedule remaining. It is difficult to see any pattern for this, and it presumably represents the effect of a whole series of *ad hoc* decisions.

29

The position has been complicated even further in recent years with the development of the so called medium edition. The first of these was the German medium edition, first published in 1967, since when the French schedules have also appeared. Proposals have also been made for an English medium edition. However, a study made in certain areas by Jack Mills showed that the *ad hoc* nature of the abbreviation from full to abridged was very obviously paralleled by the abbreviation for the medium edition; it is not possible to determine the pattern by which the full schedules are reduced to ' medium ' size.[30]

In all three editions of UDC, full, medium and abridged, it is possible to use the colon and other synthetic devices to represent syntactic relationships. The extent of the abridgement from one edition to another should therefore simply be a reflection of the length of the schedules, since abridgement is performed by leaving out terms which normally would appear in particular hierarchies. However the position is complicated by the fact that UDC, though synthetic, is not entirely analytic; there are many areas in UDC where composite subjects are enumerated, and in some places analytico-synthetic schedules have the occasional enumerative section thrown in. If we count the length of the schedules it seems clear that the relationship between the full edition and the abridgements is approximately ten to one; something like 120,000 terms enumerated to 12,000. The medium edition is intended to come roughly on the geometric mean between the two editions: that is to say, we should expect it to have something like 40,000 terms enumerated. This is approximately correct, but as has been pointed out this does not represent a systematic approach to abridgement.

One is forced to question the justification for the present methods of abridgement at either level. It is obviously useful to have a one-volume set of the schedules available, particularly when the full schedules are not available and seem unlikely to be available, as has unfortunately been the position with the full English edition until very recently. However, the development of a medium edition would seem to indicate that the abridged edition, cut down to one tenth size, has proved inadequate. Will the medium edition prove to be any more adequate? It is difficult to see a justification for it in its present role; one is forced to the conclusion that it would have been more sensible to devote the available effort to a thorough updating and revision of the existing full edition.

SUMMARY

In this chapter we have tried to trace the origins and growth of UDC from its first use by Otlet and LaFontaine to classify their 'Universal index' through its development under Donker Duyvis to its present position as one of the three major general classification schemes in world wide use. The problems which have arisen through the dependence of the scheme on the voluntary work of a limited number of people, divorced from any single large collection of literature, and the lack of a rational basis for the present three levels of detail, are indicated as topics to be discussed in more detail in subsequent chapters.

CHAPTER 3

THE PRESENT STATUS OF UDC

As has been pointed out in the previous chapter, the various editions of UDC have developed in a somewhat haphazard fashion, and if we consider the present situation we shall find limited comfort.

If we look first of all at the English edition we find, as has been mentioned in the previous chapter, that publication of the full edition began in 1943 and is expected to be completed in 1972. The first schedules were published in fairly substantial volumes; for example the whole of the Physical Sciences except Chemistry and the whole of the Biological Sciences were each published as single volumes, giving three volumes 5-53, 54, and 55-59, for the whole of Science; another example is the inclusion of all of the auxiliaries, including the rather lengthy place schedules, together with class o, Generalia, in another single volume. In recent years, the policy of publishing in very much smaller fascicules has been adopted, and while some of these are reasonably substantial, for example 616 Pathology, others may give rise to some doubt as to whether they should have been allowed to stand alone. One notable example is Customs policy 337 which consists of one page of schedules only. The complete edition is expected to occupy about ninety eight fascicules. Most of these fascicules consists of schedules and index, but this is not true of all of them; for example, the schedule for computers, 681.3, has no index, though the one page schedule referred to earlier *is* accompanied by its own index![31] Schedules are generated by translation from the German edition, followed by editing within the appropriate subject panel; the object of this is to ensure that the terminology used is correct and up to date, and in this it is usually quite successful. However, the indexing is usually done separately, and one is liable to find that there is little consistency between the indexes to different parts of the schedules. No index exists to the full schedules in English, nor, as far as one can see at present, is one planned. This would be a very considerable task, and it seems unlikely that the resources to do it would be available. There is no doubt that the lack of a single index will be a considerable hindrance to the use of the scheme; users can either try the abridged edition for a lead, or guess which of the ninety eight fascicules to look in, a hit and miss situation which is obviously unsatisfactory.[32]

It is also necessary to accept the fact that a great part of the English full edition is at present grossly out of date. The sections which were published in 1943, which included the volumes for Science and Generalia already mentioned, have of course been very considerably revised since that date, and it is necessary to study the *Extensions and corrections* carefully in order to discover the latest state of the schedules. This is in contrast with some of the other areas, for example the sections within Medicine 61, which have been translated and updated quite recently and therefore represent the current state of the schedules. There is obviously a great deal of work to be done before the full English edition will be a useful tool. The English abridged edition, first published in 1948 and most recently in 1961, is again rather out of date, but no effort is available to produce a revised version. It is likely therefore to continue to get more and more out of date as time goes by, which is a very unsatisfactory state of affairs. A number of important schedules have been introduced in the past ten years, for example the one for Computers, and these—which are likely to be used in a number of libraries—simply are not to be found in the English abridgement There have also been some recent developments in the notation for the auxiliaries; to the list found in the third English abridged edition, we now have to add the double colon and the use of hyphen 0, both of which are important recent developments.

The colon has always been regarded as a ' pivoting device '. For their Universal Index, Otlet and LaFontaine had suggested that a piece of notation consisting of two base numbers joined together by a colon should be filed under both of the numbers; this could be done by making two copies of the entry and underlining the appropriate half, so that the filing could be done by clerical staff. The convention grew up that any two numbers joined together by a colon would have entries made under both, and the need for underlining disappeared. However, there are situations in UDC in which the second part of a two part class number is relatively insignificant, and does not warrant an entry; the conventional approach in effect insists that it should be given an entry anyway. This can be rather wasteful and lead to unwanted entries, which serve merely to bulk out a catalogue and make it that much more difficult to use. The double colon has been introduced in order to indicate that the ' reversing ' technique should not be applied; if two basic class numbers are joined together by a double colon, an entry is made only under the first followed by the second, *not* under the second followed by the first in addition.

The hyphen o common sub-division has been added with one particular example in mind, –05 Persons. A Persons facet introduced by –05 has been in use in class 3 Social sciences for some years now; normally, as a special auxiliary it would have been given merely a hyphen, but obviously it was felt to be of very general application throughout the Social sciences, and the zero ensured that it filed before any other hyphen subdivisions. It is now realized that a Persons facet is one which can be of value throughout the schedules and this particular facet has therefore been transferred to the common auxiliaries. This has meant that the –o can now be used for other similar examples, such as –03 Materials, published as P70–7 and now officially adopted. Neither of these common auxiliary symbols : : and –o is to be found in the current English abridgement, nor will they be found in the trilingual supplement.

There has as yet been no effective progress on a medium edition in English, though this is certainly one of the projects which the National Committee has very much in mind. It would involve translation of the German medium edition and would thus be a fairly considerable task. However, it is possible that the experimental work carried out in the United States under the auspices of the American Institute of Physics may be of some help here. For this project R Freeman and Mrs P Atherton were obliged to produce an up to date edition of UDC; in order to do this they devised a computer program to merge existing full schedules, abridged schedules, and where necessary translations of the medium edition in German. The overall effect was to give a ' sort of ' English medium edition; this was rather a hotch potch, as may be imagined from the method of compilation, but nevertheless it functioned reasonably well in the experiments, and did give a basis for a medium edition in English. However, for one reason or another, mainly the lack of effort available within the British Standards Institution, nothing further has been done with this work, although it is available on computer readable magnetic tape.[33]

34

EDITIONS IN LANGUAGES OTHER THAN ENGLISH

The situation is not a great deal better if one considers the other editions of UDC. The second German edition started publication in 1958, but so far only class five and part of class six are available. Certainly these two classes between them occupy something over four fifths of the whole of the schedules, but even so there is clearly a great deal of work to be done. In addition, the schedules for Science, published in 1958, are now inevitably outdated in some important areas; there has for example been an important new schedule in Geology since that date.

The medium German edition was published in 1967 and is the basic source for other editions at this level. However, it is not as yet clear what the publication pattern for the medium editions will be; clearly, they will require revision at fairly regular intervals, but the revision of a medium edition is likely to take a great deal more effort than the revision of an abridged edition. There appears to be some risk that the medium edition may suffer the same fate as the full edition, in failing to maintain currency. The German abridged edition is also now considerably out of date, having reached its third edition in 1955, and would have to be supplemented by the trilingual edition of its ten year supplement.

The French seem to have given up hope altogether for their full edition. After a burst of activity at the beginning of the second world war, when Medicine 61, Engineering 62, and Business Methods 65, were all published, there was a pause until the beginning of the next decade when classes Generalia 0, Religion 2, and Social Sciences 3 were published. All six of these are now out of print and there seems to be little progress. A French medium edition has now appeared, and is the most up to date of both the French editions and the medium editions. The French abridged edition, like the German, is now even more out dated than the British, having been published in 1958. This could also be brought up to date to some extent by use of the ten year supplement to the trilingual edition, but this is at best a makeshift.

There are full editions in several other languages: Japanese, Polish, Portuguese, Russian and Spanish. Abridged editions are available in ten other languages, and we are told that medium editions are also in preparation in other languages, though as yet they have not appeared in print.

SPECIAL SUBJECT EDITIONS

One of the ways in which National Committees and the FID have tried to get round the problems of publishing full editions is through what are known as special subject editions. One of the ways in which UDC is frequently used is to classify in detail a special collection; obviously for this purpose the full schedules, if they are available, are most satisfactory to use if we are to obtain the necessary specificity. However, all special collections tend to gather round them 'fringe' collections of material which, though not falling within the category of essential to the study of the subject area in question, may well form an important part of its context. It is, for example, difficult to envisage the study of Library Science which takes no account whatever of printing. These fringe subjects will normally be present in the collection in relatively small quantities; they will not perhaps need to be indexed in such depth as the main collection. For this purpose, the schedules of the abridged edition would prove satisfactory. The special subject editions are an attempt to get the best of both worlds, by providing the full schedules for the core area, while providing only the abridged schedules for the auxiliary subjects. There are now several of these, one of the most notable being the special subject edition for Nuclear Science and Technology, prepared by the United Kingdom Atomic Energy Authority with collaboration from similar institutions in other countries.[34] Another example is that for Metallurgy, prepared by the Library of the Iron and Steel Institute in London.[35] A significant point about these special subject editions is that they normally are compiled by a particular organization; they represent very often the usage of that particular organization. While this means that they are biased, such a bias may well be not merely acceptable but welcome to a similar organization elsewhere; hence the success of the special subject editions. However, here again we see the problem of keeping up to date; there is no official mechanism for revising these editions, and their updating depends on whether the organization responsible for them in the first place feels the need for revision sufficiently urgently to be willing to devote the amount of effort necessary for its publication. It should be remembered that a tool which serves adequately within a library for its day to day work may well need considerable editing before it is acceptable to the world at large.[36]

PHYSICAL PRODUCTION OF SCHEDULES

As has already been mentioned, UDC schedules appear in a variety of physical forms. The full editions are normally published in several volumes; the German edition occupied seven volumes, together with three volumes of alphabetical index. The English full edition began on a similar pattern, but has now gone over to issue in fascicules, while the French edition started by issuing fairly substantial volumes, but has now ceased publication altogether as far as one can tell. The medium edition is normally one volume of schedules and one of index, while the abridged editions are normally in one single volume. All of these methods are open to the standard objection that they are somewhat difficult to update in practical use. In a library, the classification scheme used is a working tool, and the classifier could not tolerate a situation in which he found it necessary to look in a variety of places to make sure of what schedule he is supposed to be using. Classifiers therefore find it necessary to establish the latest version of the schedules, and then amend their master copy, probably in manuscript or typescript, in order to have an acceptable working tool. This can clearly occupy a fair amount of time, and is a continuing task; *Extensions and corrections* are published every six months, and though the progressive cumulation is normally helpful, it does mean that the classifier wishing to establish what amendments he has to make to his working copy has to study each new issue carefully to find those parts which have been added since the previous issue.

The German full edition has now introduced an interesting innovation, in that recent schedules have been published in loose leaf form. One good example of this is Engineering 62, published in 1964 and updated since. The provision of new loose leaf sheets does save the classifier quite a lot of work in maintaining his working copy up to date without the necessity for scanning the *Extensions and corrections*. However, the problem is not quite as simple as it might appear at first sight. Most libraries do build up their working copies various notes, particularly cross-references directing them to other parts of the schedules which may be relevant in particular instances; substitution of a new loose leaf sheet for the old would mean that any such notes would run the risk of being lost. It would be possible to interleave blank paper with the schedules and use this for the notes, but certainly the problem is one that should not be overlooked. A further point is of course the fact that the alphabetical index may also need fairly substantial amendment if a new schedule is published, and although the schedule itself may occupy only a few pages, the repercussions may spread throughout the alphabetical index and require very considerable amendment. One of the consequences of this is that classifiers tend to do without an adequate alphabetical index, which is in itself a severe handicap which may in effect prove insuperable. Despite many years of teaching in library schools that an alphabetical index is an essential part of a classification scheme and of any classified arrangement resulting from the use of that scheme, many libraries still do not bother to provide this essential tool; surprise is then expressed that the users seem not to want to make use of the catalogue.

Wellisch has suggested a radically new way of publishing amendments to the UDC as long ago as 1960,[37] and has recently suggested that without a revision of its management structure there is little hope of the publication of UDC ever improving sufficiently to make it acceptable. His proposals are discussed in chapter 4. It is certainly the case at the moment that the publication methods of UDC and its physical presentation are tolerated rather than accepted by users.

One way out of the dilemma might be the use of computers to produce updated versions of the schedules. The work of Rigby[38] and of Freeman and Atherton[33] in the United States, and AWRE[39] in Great Britain has shown clearly that production of the UDC schedules by computer is feasible; there may be some loss where the notation does not accurately reflect the hierarchical structure, but in general this is found to affect only part of the overall schedules. A computer can be made to select a type face appropriate to the hierarchical level by programming it to recognize the length of a given piece of notation, and the results can be quite satisfactory. As yet, no one appears to have studied the potential of COM (Computer Output Microfilm), but this could well be a useful addition to the tools at our disposal. As more and more libraries obtain the equipment necessary for using this particular physical form of material, we are likely to see a considerable increase in its use, and the success of the publication of 'Books in English' and the Westminster City Library catalogue has shown that this is a very satisfactory method for the librarian's own tools.[40] The cost of COM is small compared with the cost of comparable printout by conventional means, and users of UDC might well be prepared to subscribe to a continuous updating service in this medium. The cheapness of the method would mean that the index could be updated as well as the schedules without involving the user in an intolerable financial outlay. If the full schedules were available in this way, it would be interesting to find out how many librarians would continue to use any of the shorter versions. The latter could of course also be made available in the same way.

INTELLECTUAL CONTENT OF THE SCHEDULES

So far we have discussed the availability of the schedules in physical form. Although there is no doubt that the physical problems of obtaining the schedules and of maintaining them in an up to date working condition are very important, librarians would be willing to exert the necessary effort if the schedules themselves were worth having, and better for their purpose than other existing schemes. We have therefore to consider whether the schedules as they stand at present are in fact satisfactory, and if not, in what ways they may be criticized. There are a number of approaches one can make to this particular aspect.

BIAS IN THE SCHEDULES

Dewey's original Decimal Classification was intended to be used in the Library of Amherst College, and reflected to a very large extent the literary warrant of that College. Some amendments were made in the second edition to make the scheme more generally acceptable, but there is no doubt that, by and large, the overall structure of Dewey to this day reflects quite strongly its origins in a small American University Library. UDC, having been based on the fifth edition of Dewey, inevitably carried over the basic structure with all its faults and prejudices. Although considerable efforts have been made to reduce or eliminate this bias, these have not been entirely successful, and there are some areas in which it would appear to be difficult to see how bias could be avoided entirely.

The classic example of bias in Dewey is almost certainly religion. Dewey, when he spoke of religion meant the Christian religion; other religions were, if not quite myths, then at least rather less worthy of serious consideration than Christianity. UDC is intended for a world wide audience, and such an obvious bias would be totally unacceptable in many parts of the world; the attempt to eliminate this bias has been achieved to some extent, in that schedules for other religions are now reasonably well developed, but it is not possible without a very considerable alteration of the overall structure of UDC to eliminate the inequality in the allocation of notation. Six two digit numbers are allocated to Christianity; one to all other religions. The present author has discussed elsewhere the kinds of anomaly that arise in all classification schemes in relation to women and similar subjects, and it is not proposed to repeat those examples here.[41] Other examples are easy to find; for example if we look at the schedule for classes of persons in

39

Political Science in UDC we find an extraordinary progression which has serious implications for those of us who are civil servants or ministers of religion:

323.3	Social Groups and Strata, Ranks, Vocations
323.31	Nobility, Upper Classes
323.32	Bourgeoisie, Middle Class, Peasantry, The Independent Professions
323.33	Employees. Workers
323.34	Slaves. Serfs
323.35	Clergy
323.37	Officials

New schedules can display a degree of bias, despite the firm intention of the editors to avoid this. This is perhaps an inevitable reflection of the fact that systems differ throughout the world; a good example is Education, where the relatively recent schedule compiled in Germany, and reflecting the educational structure of that country, has proved quite unsuitable for use in British libraries, because of the quite different educational structure in this country. If we add to this the trivial but nevertheless real differences in terminology which may occur in different countries, it can be seen that great care needs to be taken if a 'neutral' schedule is to result. Again taking an example from Education, most people are aware of the peculiar British use of the term 'Public' School to mean the reverse; to fit this into a classification schedule would indeed cause problems if it were to be used both in this country and, say, in the United States! Users of DC are already well aware of some of the problems of American terminology that occur in that scheme; it is only the fact that UDC is at present little used in the United States that has prevented this kind of problem from becoming serious in the past. If the use of UDC were to spread to the USA, this kind of difference might well prove to be a serious hindrance to its use there.

OVERALL INTELLECTUAL PATTERN OF SCHEDULES

The overall structure of Dewey's Decimal Classification has remained unchanged since the second edition, published in 1885. Dewey recognized very early that librarians would not welcome a scheme which involved them in frequent changes, with all the administrative work this would involve, and though there were some fairly substantial changes between the first and second editions, with the latter Dewey laid down the principle of 'integrity of numbers': the meaning of a particular piece of notation would not be changed, though a heading might be expanded and new headings might be inserted round it at previously unused notations. This meant, of course, that the structure of the scheme was fixed in broad outline and could not be changed, since all the three-figure notation had been allocated. The pattern adopted by UDC was thus the one adopted by Dewey in the 1880's, and just as Dewey has remained within this framework, so has UDC.

Dewey's outline reflected the literary warrant of Amherst College, a not particularly large American University with a strong bias towards the Humanities. He divided the whole of knowledge into nine main classes, with a tenth for 'Generalia'—works on knowledge as a whole, or those which would not fit comfortably into any of the other nine, *eg* Works remarkable for the nature of their content; a polite expression for the 'curiosa' beloved of certain booksellers. He made no claims for logical order in his main classes; except insofar as it was based on 'the inverted Baconian arrangement of the St. Louis library . . .', his order did not attempt to reflect any philosophical approach. Indeed, it is difficult to see how one can seriously relate his order to the very broad divisions put forward by Bacon, even if they are inverted:

> History
> Poesie
> Philosophy

becoming

> Philosophy
> Poesie
> History

which in Dewey becomes

> (Generalia)
> Philosophy
> Religion
> Social sciences
> Philology
> Science
> Useful arts
> Fine arts
> Literature
> History

Unless one assumes that the first six all fall into the same group Philosophy, the relationship is obscure. There are certain peculiarities in the order, obvious enough to us but perhaps not so to Dewey; we would not wish to separate Philology and Literature, and History is too far removed from its companion social sciences. UDC still reflects, as does DC, this outline, with one or two minor changes, such as the transfer of Philology to a new heading Literature and Philology, which brings together these two related areas, or if necessary can give parallel divisions under each specific language. Far more sweeping changes were proposed in 1963, but have met with little acceptance by users; these suggested the grouping of Humanities at the beginning of a revised table, followed by the Social Sciences, then by Science and Technology. Objections to these changes have been based not on their intellectual implications but on the practical difficulties inherent in the use of notation in a classification scheme.

NOTATIONAL PROBLEMS

Any systematic arrangement of subjects must be accompanied by a notation of some kind to make it usable; it would not be tolerable if one had to search through the system each time one wanted to find a particular heading, so each topic is given a piece of notation showing its place in the overall order, and an alphabetical index is provided to lead enquirers to the appropriate piece of notation. In practical everyday use, notation is placed on catalogue cards, the backs of books, and various other records, and represents a considerable investment of time and money. To alter the main class order of a scheme such as UDC would involve altering the notation on large numbers of documents, as well as moving the actual documents to their new location and changing all the records; small wonder that librarians already facing a considerable day to day effort in maintaining their collections in classified order are more than reluctant to change it.

With UDC, the problem is exacerbated by the bias towards the Humanities already referred to in Dewey's original outline. Dewey allocated one fifth of the one-digit notation to Science and Technology 5 and 6, and UDC retains this allocation. However, some four fifths of UDC schedules fall into these two classes; in the English abridged edition, the number of pages occupied by each class is as follows:

1	philosophy	30-32 (3)
2	religion	32-36 (3+)
3	social sciences, law, education	36-57 (21+)
4	philology, linguistics	57-59 (2)
5	mathematics and natural science	59-79 (20)

6 applied science and technology	80-134 (54)
7 arts, entertainment and sport	134-142 (8+)
8 literature, belles-lettres	142-143 (1)
9 geography, biography, history	143-145 (2)

giving a total of seventy four pages for science and technology, forty for all the rest, but when it is remembered that many of the science and technology schedules (*eg* Medicine) are greatly abridged, whereas this is not true to the same extent of the rest, it can be seen that the disproportion is noteworthy. Sixty five per cent of the abridged schedules are crammed into twenty per cent of the notational base.

The problem is compounded by the fact that it is in science and technology that most new developments occur, and in which new and, more significantly, expanded schedules are required. This is of course demonstrated to a degree in the present inequality of allocation; if all subjects expanded at the same rate, Dewey's allocation would still be equitable. It is however growing rapidly more acute in that while development in the humanities is very slow, and in social sciences is only now beginning to accelerate, in science and technology expansion appears to be following an exponential curve, so that the present allocation is likely to grow even less adequate as time goes by.

The proposed revision of UDC would have gathered everything except science and technology into classes 0 and 1, or 0, 1 and 2, leaving all the rest for science and technology. Such large scale changes proved to be quite unacceptable to the vast majority of UDC users, and the only one to be implemented has been the transfer of philology already mentioned. Not many libraries classified by UDC have very much material in this area, one assumes. The other proposals appear to have been quietly forgotten, particularly in recent months, when more exciting prospects have presented themselves in the shape of a possible 'roof' classification for UNISIST, examined in detail in chapter 4. Before proceeding further it is important to consider UDC policy for the re-use of notation. Dewey made a rule that no piece of notation should be re-used with a different meaning, and though this rule has been gradually eroded since the fifteenth edition in 1951 it is still very largely true. UDC was always envisaged as a more flexible scheme, and its bias towards science and technology was turned to account with the introduction of the ten year starvation policy. A piece of notation which has been superseded by a new schedule is to be left unused for ten years; at the end of that time it may be used again with a completely new meaning. Any major change in the overall outline could thus prove to be a practical proposition if only there were some vacant notation in which to build up the required new schedules, though it would necessarily be a long term project. This is the argument behind the transfer of Philology to Class 8; Class 4 can now, after the required ten year period, be redeveloped in any way that appears useful. One of the more likely looking ideas, and one that has been pursued to some extent already, is the use of this piece of notation for some of those ' bridging ' Sciences such as Communications, which fall naturally between the Social Sciences and Natural Sciences. Whether there are enough of these to justify a whole one digit block of notation is not clear; one gets the feeling that notation in this class would be allocated very liberally, in contrast to the dense notation necessarily used in some of the Engineering schedules. Some of the subjects which at present are found in Science and Technology, at least partially, could be transferred to this bridging area, but it would not appear that any relief would be very great. It does seem that a complete re-structuring would be necessary if UDC is to have a modern outline. Such re-structuring, and the notational changes that this will involve, appear to be unacceptable to the people who would be involved in making the changes; a dilemma which faces every classification scheme which endeavours to keep pace with changes in knowledge.

The Americans have ' solved ' the problem by avoiding it. UDC has never been at all well known in the States and there are very few libraries using it, one of the most notable being the Engineering Societies Library in New York. When the Americans needed a classification of the broad type proposed by UNISIST, they were obliged to develop their own; at least, they felt obliged to do so, though it is fairly clear that UDC was never seriously considered except by the American Institute of Physics. The result of the American deliberations was the COSATI Subject Categories,[42] a list of subjects corresponding to a fairly broad classification scheme. It is fairly clear that these categories do not in fact represent any very great advance on the comparable UDC schedules, and some comparisons are shown in Appendix A.

DETAIL WITHIN THE SCHEDULES

When we come to examine individual schedules, we find the peculiar mixture of enumeration and synthesis that has already been mentioned in chapter 1. The original UDC schedules contained some anomalies because Dewey's schedules contained such anomalies; unfortunately schedules developed even quite recently can still contain unsatisfactory examples, where analysis has not been carried out properly, with the consequence that a schedule gives the user a mixture of enumeration and synthesis with all the possibilities of cross classification that this implies. Analysis into facets is not consistent; the present author has drawn attention to the anomaly which occurs in the schedules for Sewage Treatment, where in the middle of various kinds of treatment, *ie* activities, we find ' sludge ', *ie* a product of one of these activities.[43] Another example is to be found in a new schedule for Geology, where in the list of rocks arranged by method of formation we find a heading ' roofing slate ', *ie* a material specified by its use. These anomalies cannot occur if the basic principles of facet analysis are understood and applied, but this has not been the case in the past, and until recently the guide lines for the revision of UDC contained no reference to this kind of problem. The most recent issue of this document does indeed give the schedule compiler some information about facet analysis but does not carry this far enough.[22] Unfortunately, many of the users of UDC are completely ignorant of, and indeed one may say hostile to, modern classification theory, and schedules compiled by them, though no doubt perfectly adequate in as far as subject specification is concerned, are not necessarily very good examples of classification schedule compilation.

Anomalies in the use of the auxiliary sub-divisions have already been mentioned, as has their confusion and overlap with the point of view numbers. The proposals put forward by Schmidt and Dahlberg for the revision of UDC, discussed in chapter 4, contained certain proposals for the revision of the auxiliaries, in particular the point of view numbers. One interesting suggestion that has been put forward here is the substitution of, say, letters instead of the present arbitrary symbols used for facet indicators for the auxiliaries; computers have great difficulty in recognizing and handling the present set of symbols, and letters would be a great deal easier in this respect, as was first shown by Freeman and Atherton.[33]

SUMMARY

The present chapter has attempted to discuss the current status of UDC from a variety of points of view, ranging from the physical production of the schedules and their publication methods to the intellectual content. There is no doubt that UDC is rapidly approaching a crisis point, if indeed it has not already reached it. Developments in information retrieval and in the information to be retrieved means that any classification scheme has to move with the times if it is to continue to function adequately; one may doubt whether UDC in its present state is able to move sufficiently quickly, or at all. It is certainly true that any classification scheme used by large numbers of librarians will be faced with substantial problems if it does attempt to introduce major changes, but we may take heart from the experience of the *Decimal classification* in the United States, where the appearance of each of the three most recent editions, sixteenth, seventeenth, and eighteenth, has been greeted with cries of dismay but has nevertheless been accepted and adopted.[44]

CHAPTER 4

CURRENT DEVELOPMENTS: IDEAS FOR THE FUTURE OF UDC

There has been a great deal of discussion in recent years about future trends in UDC, questioning the basis on which the scheme has been developed so far. This questioning is healthy, for an acceptance of what has been done in the past may in fact lead a classification scheme to stagnate rather than progress with changes in the structure of knowledge. It is appropriate to look in rather more detail at some of the changes that have been proposed, including one or two that have already been mentioned in passing. The main problem remains, of course, the fact that a classification scheme must be accepted by its users if it is to survive; there will obviously have to be considerable care in determining the direction of future changes, and political motives may well play as important a part as classification theory in planning new developments. This would appear to the purist to be an abdication of responsibility, but if one is trying to develop an existing scheme, one owes a debt to the existing users, which must be considered very seriously. Current ideas have fallen into two different areas: the first of these concerns changes in the schedules and notation; the second, changes in the management structure of the editorial board of UDC, leading to changes in methods of revision and publication. These two areas will now be examined.

SECTION A: SCHEDULES AND NOTATION

The changes in the schedules and notation cannot really be taken separately since, as was shown in the past chapter, the two are often inextricably intertwined. One has also to take into account that for many of the people using UDC, ' classification ' means allocating a class

47

number to a book; what might be regarded by the purist as nothing more than subject *specification*. In UDC, one sees the medium taken for the message[45] all too clearly; the notation is regarded as the classification, instead of being merely an appendage, intended to make the use of the schedules easier. This is reflected in the fact that many of the people concerned with the revision of UDC have, it seems, no idea whatever of classification theory, and regard the construction of new schedules as being merely a way of getting ' numbers '. This is the American ' mark and park '; the belief expressed very well in a letter to *Library journal* in the words ' after all, isn't classification just a shelf location?'.[46] The present author has pointed out that if we are to take shelf classification seriously, then it has to be a great deal more than just a shelf location.[47] The implications of this for UDC have perhaps not always been realized by its users.

There is no doubt that the present notation used by UDC is clumsy. It involves a number of symbols, used as facet indicators, which have no ordinal significance, and which therefore have to be given an arbitrary filing sequence. There is also the point that these symbols represent in effect the combination order for facets and that this combination order should be linked with the filing order if the principle of inversion is to be followed. This particular principle has been discussed at length elsewhere,[48] and it is possible to say that its importance has been exaggerated; nevertheless, it is true that it is only by following the principle of inversion that one obtains a sequence in which special consistently follows general.[49] UDC notation also presents problems if we are thinking of mechanization, since it is difficult to program a computer to realize that .o has a quite different significance from .oo, and that neither of them must be confused with o on its own. The colon in UDC is also used for a variety of purposes; it is certainly a convenient piece of notation, but the question arises as to whether it is precise enough for the kind of development we have in mind.

One of the problems that arises with these arbitrary symbols, but which reflects perhaps a more general problem of classification, is the question of bonding between different elements of a composite class number. If we talk about British Proton Synchrotrons, then we recognize that it is the proton synchrotrons which are British. When we translate this into a class number, there is a danger that in a machine searching situation it would become difficult to recognize this relationship, and we might instead find ourselves retrieving information on British protons, which conjures up an interesting picture. This suggests that there should be some kind of hierarchy of combination, just as there is for the arithmetic signs in a computer formula. This point has been investigated in considerable detail by Caless[50] and Perreault,[51] from slightly different points of view. Caless pointed out that we could regard any UDC number as an example of a general formula

$$M1 \; S1 \; M2 \; S2 \; S3 \; M3 \; S4 \; S5 \; S6 \text{ etc,}$$

in which M represents a basic class number and S represents an auxiliary. We have to consider the kind of situation where S3 is related not only to M2 but also to M1, and to devise some formal means of expressing the various bonds in such a way that they can be recognized. A convention for showing the precedence to be given to the various UDC combining symbols was drawn up by Perreault, and modified in discussion later to give the following result

$$n'n \quad n/n \quad n+ \left\{ \begin{array}{l} .on \\ -n \end{array} \right. \quad \left\{ \begin{array}{l} n::n \\ .oon \end{array} \right. \quad \left\{ \begin{array}{l} (=n) \\ (n) \\ \text{``n''} \end{array} \right. \quad n:n \quad (on) \quad =n$$

where the order of precedence decreases from left to right. For example, in the class number $5/6(038)=30$, we consider first the stroke, then the parentheses and finally the equals, to give the meaning ' German language technical dictionaries of science and technology '; we do *not* relate the form first, then the extension, which would give only a very limited part of technology—up to and including 6(038) technical dictionaries.

Using this table of precedence we can see how it is possible to link together units of a composite UDC number in unambiguous fashion; in effect, to know which belongs to which. In order to override the standard linking, which will be necessary in cases where the relationships are not the straightforward ones implied by the order of appearance of elements in the class number, the use of square brackets is suggested. In the abridged English edition of 1961 the use of square brackets is tied to the idea of ' subordination '; a concept can be shown as subordinate by the use of square brackets rather than the colon, and in this situation no entry will be made under the subordinate heading. Square brackets are also suggested as a method of intercalation, giving in effect the possibility of changing the citation order in those situations where the colon is used, by converting it to a symbol which opens and closes, instead of merely indicating the beginning of a piece of notation. This method of intercalation can already be used with other indicators such as parentheses and quotation marks, both of which effectively delimit an element of notation, but it cannot be used with other facet indicators which merely denote the beginning of a notational element. However, this use of square brackets has now been abandoned in favour of use of algebraic grouping suggested by Perreault, and its place for subordination purposes has been taken by the double colon. No substitute has been proposed for purposes of intercalation. The convention finally considered by CCC in 1969 was as follows:

(10)	(9)	(8)	(7)	(6)	(5)	(4)	(3)	(2)	(1)
[ ]	n'n	n/n	n+n {	.on / −n	{ n::n / .oon	{(=n) / (n) / "n"	n:n	(on)	=n

where the numbers in parentheses above each UDC combination signify the combining precedence relative to the others.

Perreault's proposal was not enthusiastically received by all those who considered it, and was criticized by Wellisch on the grounds that it did not lead to an unambiguous result in every situation.[52] Perreault was also criticized by Wellisch for not giving translations into words of all his examples, and this is indeed a valid point. It is easy to juggle with UDC numbers to demonstrate ways in which the various indicators may be used to combine notational elements, but many of the resulting combinations will be quite meaningless and have no significance whatever in real life. Since there are certainly real life situations where UDC numbers are ambiguous, it is a pity if a proposal of this kind should be rejected on these grounds, but there is no doubt that real examples would make the case very much stronger.

Wellisch points out that there are in fact two kinds of symbol to be considered, of which only one needs a bonding rule. Non-detachable auxiliaries, to use Wellisch's term, cannot be used alone and must be added to main numbers at the right hand end; on their own, they are meaningless. These include the following:

/	Stroke
−	Hyphenated auxiliaries
.0	Special auxiliaries
.00	Points of view
'	(Synthetic device)
::	(Irreversible relation)

Since these auxiliaries cannot be used alone, no bonding rule is necessary, and we can concentrate on the 'detachable' auxiliaries, *ie* those which do have a meaning on their own and may be added to any UDC number. These are:

=1/=9   Language

(o . . .)	form
" . . ."	time
(=1/=9)	race and nationality
(1/9)	place

All of these have their own intrinsic meaning, and may be added to a simple number at the end—the usual place—or at the beginning (to bring together particular bibliographical forms, for example). They may also be intercalated, to give a change in citation order if that is thought useful. An example frequently quoted is 329 Political parties, where the normal citation order would give 329.14(42) for the Labour Party; more useful is the intercalated 329(42)14, which groups British (and other national) political parties together. In order to intercalate language or to use it at the beginning of a string, the equals sign is doubled, *eg* =30=; thus, if it were thought useful to bring together all translations of Shakespeare into German and then to subarrange by work, the notation might be:

820"15"SHAK=30=. . .

It will be noted that all the other symbols in this group are already self-contained.

Wellisch then gives the simple rule: any element in a complex UDC code specifies the elements written at its left side up to but not including any relational sign that may precede that element. If an element is to specify more than one element to its left side (two or more main numbers linked by colon or any other relational sign), the whole group of elements to be specified must be enclosed in square brackets. Similarly, if subgroups within a larger group have to be specified by an element, they must also be enclosed in square brackets. It should be noted here that by 'relational sign' Wellisch means in effect only the colon, since he deprecates the use of the plus sign. (In his examples, Wellisch replaces the plus sign by the colon; this appears to be a retrograde step, since there is a difference between A *and* B and A *in relation to* B. The best way of replacing the plus sign is by making more than one entry; this avoids introducing further ambiguity into the meaning of the colon.

For instance, one of Wellisch's examples is

[[05 : 32] : [07 : 8]](72)

for which the meaning 'Political periodicals and literary journalism in Mexico' is given. Using the colon, one is forced to assume that a relationship, some kind of interaction, between political periodicals and literary journalism is implied, whereas this is not necessarily implicit in the word 'and'. If the document in question does indeed deal with two similar subjects without any interaction, it is better to give it two class numbers, though we shall of course still need square brackets:

[05 : 32](72)

[07 : 8](72)

In view of the problems found by Freeman and Atherton in using the colon, it would appear to be ill-advised to burden it with yet another meaning, particularly one which is semantically very weak.)

The use of square brackets for algebraic grouping in this way has now been officially adopted by UDC,[53] but whether it is widely used is another matter; one has the feeling that for most UDC users it is more of a frill than an essential.

RELATIONAL NOTATION

In addition to his work on the use of square brackets, Perreault has put forward a detailed proposal for a scheme of 'relators' which would serve to clarify the ambiguities inherent in the use of the colon.[54] The complete scheme is extremely complex, and represents a considerable analytical effort. Perreault sees relationships between concepts falling into six major types:

a) ordinal
b) determinative
c) attributive
d) interactive
e) subsumptive
f) logical

Within each major heading, detailed subdivision may be carried out, and Perreault tends to adopt a triadic approach; for example, for a) he gives the following suggestions:

time: before, simultaneous, after
size: smaller, equal, larger
degree: equivalent, inferior, superior
position: lateral, axial, vertical

The last of these may itself be further divided:

lateral: right, centre, left
axial: front, centre, back
vertical: above, level, below

Within b) we find a similar tripartition, into active, interactive and passive. The same kind of relationship can occur in more than one place, depending on one's point of view; for example, we find under 'active' the concept 'destructive' with a subdivision 'injuring': (using Perreault's notation, as circulated by FID)

e   Determinative
ea   Active
eai   Destructive
eaid   Injuring

We also find a similar concept under 'interactive' and 'passive':

eb   Interactive
ebi   Contrary
ebid   Attack

ec   Passive
eci   Destroyed
ecid   Injured

We might thus end up with several different ways in which to express a particular nexus of concepts:

633.11 ecid 632.693.2   Wheat crops injured by rats   (passive)
632.693.2 eaid 633.11   Rats injuring wheat crops   (active)
632.693.2 ebid 633.11   Rats attacking wheat crops   (interactive)

Some of these problems were noted by Perreault, who modified his schema before it was circulated by FID in 1968. For example, though it is possible to say that if A is below B, then B is above A, a similar antithesis does not exist in all circumstances; 'A is favourable to B' does not carry any implications about the effect of B on A. Such relationships can only be expressed in one way. In some cases, the classifier is expected to make a value judgment; in the example given above, we may expect a measure of agreement that rats do indeed attack wheat injuriously, but how sure could we be that similar agreement would be reached if the question were one of 'favourable attitude'? Symbiosis is subsumed under Interactive:

e   Determinative
eb   Interactive
ebg   Concordant
ebgd   Association; Community; Symbiosis

whereas Parasitism falls into a different category:

e   Determinative
eb   Interactive
ebh   Differing
ebhd   Borrowing; Parasitism; Instrumentality; Utilization

However, Parasitism is defined as a form of Symbiosis;[55] and, to pursue the matter further, would not Parasitism be regarded as coming under the heading 'Contrary' rather than merely 'Differing'? In the extreme case, parasitism leads to the death of the host, which suggests a rather more aggressive relationship than merely Utilization:

ebi   Contrary
ebid   Attack; Aggression

The above comments may, in a sense, be regarded as picking on points of detail which may be corrected by revision; there is a more serious objection to the use of such detailed schemes: their effect on the costs of information retrieval. It is fairly obvious that they add to input costs, by making it that much more difficult to classify the subject matter of a document; they may also add to output costs, by making a search that much more difficult also. Results from a number of studies have indicated, to put it no more strongly, that the use of relationships (*eg* roles) tends to decrease recall rather seriously without giving a worthwhile increase in relevance.[56] Work at the College of Librarianship Wales on Farradane's system of relational operators gave somewhat inconclusive results; only thirteen per cent of the searches carried out were affected by the use of the operators and of these, the improvement (which one would have expected) was very small in most cases—certainly not enough to justify the very considerable increase in indexing time required.[57]

Perreault's schema of relators has been published by FID as an 'optional extra', to be assessed over a period of a few years. In general, it would seem that it is unlikely to win any very great acceptance. Many of the concepts listed are already available in UDC, though admittedly in a scattered fashion; for example, in the common auxiliaries we find .004.6 Deterioration, "71" Developmental stages, (−191) Inside, while in the special auxiliaries for 62 Engineering we find −181 Dimensions. One cannot envisage any large scale acceptance of the system except perhaps as part of a thorough and much more general revision. Furthermore, the work done in PRECIS and discussed later suggests that it is possible to index in depth without using more than about a dozen relationships of a fairly high degree of generality.

There is also a minor notational problem. Perreault allocated a letter notation, but used only the letters a to i, so that it is quite feasible to replace them by figures. To do so would however lead to confusion with basic UDC numbers unless some kind of delimiter is introduced. Three suggestions were put forward: the first was to use the letters as they stood, avoiding confusion but introducing a new kind of symbol (lower case letters); the second was to use a double symbol :)...(: *eg* 633.11 :)5394(: 632.693.2, which would have the advantages of placing the relator table immediately after the colon in the schedules; while the third was to use –001.../–009...: *eg* 633.11–005395:632.693.2 which departs from the UDC practice of never having more than three symbols without some form of punctuation to break them up into manageable units.

The two proposals discovered so far have assumed that the main basis of UDC would remain unchanged; that improvements would need to be grafted on to the existing stock. Other proposals for revision have suggested much more far-reaching reforms, some of which would lead to the disappearance of UDC as we know it today.

REFORM OF THE SCHEDULES: PRESSURE FROM UNISIST

In 1967 a joint central committee was set up by Unesco and ICSU to carry out a feasibility study of a world science information system, to be named UNISIST.[58] Pressure for this development came from a variety of directions, perhaps two of these being the most significant. The first is the traditional respect for the free interchange of scientific information, essential if science is to maintain its consensus of ' public knowledge ', as Ziman has termed it.[59] As science has grown in the post-war years, with the growth of new nations, so the need for improved methods of communication has become apparent; together with the growth of this need the world has seen an unprecedented growth in communications technology, such that traditional means of communication run a risk of being left behind. In these circumstances, international effort on the grand scale is the only possible solution if we are to avoid choking the channels of communication and hindering or perhaps even halting the growth of new knowledge *and its diffusion*. Preliminary meetings of the UNISIST working party restricted their studies very largely to ' conventional ' means of disseminating scientific information: journals, abstracts and indexes, libraries, etc. Other methods were considered to be outside its terms of reference, though in view of the pressures which led to its formation this appears to have been a rather narrow view.

The second direction from which pressure has already become significant is economics. The increasing quantity of scientific information to be disseminated, and the increase in the number of significant sources, has led to the development of various cooperative efforts. Perhaps the first of these was in the field of nuclear physics and engineering, where the lead was taken shortly after the war by the United States. The US Atomic Energy Commission was given as one of its objectives the dissemination to as wide an audience as possible of all unclassified (*ie* security unclassified) information within its field; this it did through two major efforts: Nuclear Science Abstracts, and 'deposit libraries' of technical reports. Nuclear Science Abstracts endeavoured to cover the whole of the world's literature, and by the early 1960's the USAEC Technical Information Division was finding it difficult to keep up with the ever increasing quantities, without increasing its budget to an unrealistic level. Help was sought from similar bodies throughout the world, *eg* the United Kingdom Atomic Energy Authority and Euratom, and NSA is now produced by a considerable cooperative effort.[60]

Similar trends have become obvious in other scientific fields. In the United Kingdom, OSTI have supported the setting up of a number of specialized information centres, *eg* the crystallographic data centre at Cambridge, on the grounds that a need exists which can only be met by the expenditure of funds by the community at large, to support this vital function of disseminating information. One may also mention here the agreements by which *Chemical abstracts* has become the major service in its field for the English-speaking world, with *Science abstracts* serving a similar end in the field of physics.

If a world scientific information system is to be set up, then clearly one of its requirements will be some kind of indexing language which is widely acceptable to its members. Recommendation 4 relates to this:

'The attention of scientists, learned societies, and information science associations should be drawn to the need for joint efforts in developing better tools for the control and conversion of natural and indexing languages in science and technology. UNISIST adherents should be invited in particular to consider the initiation of a few pilot projects, under the sponsorship of scientific organizations, aimed at testing new methodological and organizational devices in this respect, with a special emphasis on international and interdisciplinary requirements.'

The use of UDC for this purpose was mentioned, with the comments that 'its further potential has yet to be realized' and 'further studies and experiments to test its applicability to retrieval systems are desirable'. However, a study by Aslib of the various universal systems available came to the conclusion that UDC was no more than the best of a rather poor bunch, though one has to moderate this criticism when it appears that only part of UDC was looked at in any detail because of the lack of published schedules.[61] (This merely confirms what has already been stated: that a classification scheme which is not published in a satisfactory manner cannot be a successful scheme.) It was clear that to a large number of people concerned with UNISIST, UDC as it stood was not acceptable, and this has led to two rather different solutions being put forward for consideration.

REVISION WITHIN THE PRESENT FRAMEWORK

Revision of UDC schedules is a continuing process, as was made clear earlier; however, the objective has always been to introduce new material with the minimum of change, on the grounds that major changes would inconvenience users. Changes have also been piecemeal —although it has been the intention to edit every new proposal carefully and remove from it anything inconsistent with existing UDC practice, in the event a great many inconsistencies have inevitably made their way into the schedules. Some examples of this kind of anomaly have already been discussed in chapter 3. One way of producing a more satisfactory classification scheme would be to remove these anomalies by large scale editing combined with notational rationalization. Proposals along these lines have been put forward by A F Schmidt, in a paper submitted to the FID Working Group for UNISIST in 1971.[62] Schmidt puts forward two slightly different proposals for notational revision, both of which would achieve the desired objective of giving clearer differentiation than is now possible between different forms of subdivision or synthesis. In the first, division of main numbers directly, *ie* hierarchically within the primary facet, would be by figures following directly after a point, a hyphen or an apostrophe; special auxiliaries, *ie* facets specific to a subject (other than the primary facet), would be introduced by the same three indicators followed by a single zero; and common auxiliaries, *ie* those which may be used anywhere, would be introduced by one of the three indicators followed by two zeroes. In the second proposal, direct subdivisions would all use a point, special auxiliaries would all use the apostrophe, and common auxiliaries the hyphen, followed in each case by 1 to 9, 01 to 09, or 001 to 009 as required. The second possibility would appear to be more helpful in that it would involve less confusion between the use of the different symbols. In addition to these symbols, the already existing indicators would be used for language, form, place, race and time (Wellisch's 'detachable' auxiliaries); square brackets would be used for algebraic grouping; and the + would be redefined as coordination. Some new symbols would be introduced: the circumflex is to be used to indicate synthesis (though no indication is given of how, or in what circumstances); ! would be used to indicate re-use of notation within the ten year period; * would be used to indicate that notation from some other system is being used; and finally, a bar over a piece of notation would show the cancellation of that particular schedule, eg $\overline{621.384.61}$.

FUNDAMENTAL RECONSTRUCTION

Far more radical proposals for revision have been put forward by Mrs I Dahlberg.[63] The choice of title 'Possibilities for a new universal decimal classification' indicates that the changes proposed are so radical that the result would in effect be a new classification; indeed, the author points out: 'the chief advantage must be seen in the fact that it is simpler to build up an entirely new classification system than to satisfactorily revise an existing one'. Mrs Dahlberg would replace the existing structure by one based on a recent analysis by C F von Weizäcker,[64] with the following main classes:

1 Structural sciences
      (eg mathematics, cybernetics, information theory)
2 Physics, chemistry, geo-sciences and technology
      (eg astrophysics, geology, mineralogy, oceanography)
3 Biology
      (eg botany, zoology, biophysics, biochemistry)
4 Applied biological sciences
      (eg human and veterinary medicine, agriculture)
5 Anthropology (man and his earth)
      (eg ethnology, history, geography, psychology)
6 Social sciences (man among his equals)
      (eg politics, law, education, leisure activities)
7 Engineering
      (eg transportation, construction, process engineering)
8 Information sciences
      (eg museology, library science, communication)
9 Humanities
      (eg literature, arts, music, philosophy, religion)
Within each of these main classes, subdivision would be limited to

what Mrs Dahlberg calls 'subfields of subject fields'; the terminology (translated from the original German) is not clear, but presumably this implies that division of a subject field is restricted to the primary facet. For example, *ethics* is an acceptable subfield of *philosophy*, and *architecture* of *arts;* this would appear to be the kind of approach found in Colon Classification, where these divisions are found before the first round Personality facet. It is not clear at what point one draws the line; is *temperance* a legitimate subfield of *ethics,* or does it fall into 'a mere facet'? There is obviously little to be gained by quibbles over terminology, but the point is a real one; at what stage does division cease to be division into true subject fields? In many cases, the answer must be based on tradition: the 'canonical' division of Ranganathan. We have not yet carried our analysis far enough to be able to recognize underlying patterns, though the work of the Classification Research Group, discussed later, has been of help.

However, if one studies the proposed main classes, it is clear that they present almost as many anomalies and unsatisfactory collocations as the present ones. It is not clear quite what is meant by technology in class 2; what *is* clear is that it is as widely separated from Engineering in class 7 as the two are in the Bibliographic Classification,[65] yet a major trend in modern technology has been its increasing use of 'scientific techniques', to the extent that it becomes difficult at times to distinguish the two at all. The present author has discussed the problems of classification in science and technology in a paper reprinted as Appendix B; it is clear that the proposal reviewed here would merely accentuate this particular difficulty. Psychology in 5 is separated from medicine in 4 and education in 6; its already tenuous links with philosophy (in 9) must evidently be totally severed. The whole outline bears a resemblance to that put forward by Bliss, with a few concessions to modern ideas; it is just as open to severe criticism as the present outline of UDC, and certainly would not appear to justify the effort needed to implement the necessary changes.

The proposal then continues with suggestions for improvements in the organization of the special auxiliaries, to give a degree of consistency in their use. It has already been demonstrated in chapter 3 that the present organization leaves much to be desired; the emphasis there was on notational inconsistencies and confusion between special and common auxiliaries, but closer study reveals a complete lack of any standard approach to the construction of facets, even for similar subjects. Mrs Dahlberg therefore suggests the following guidelines:

.01	Theoretical principles
.02	Objects in a subject field (parts, components, etc)
.03	Processes (techniques, methods, actions, etc)
.04	Attributes (accidentals, properties, characteristics features, etc)
.05	left vacant for the time being
.06	Order (organization, orientation, status, etc)
.07	Relations (internal, external, etc)
.08	Determination (function, influence, effect, use, etc)
.09	Evaluation (rating, etc)

This outline is stated to be based on classification of general terms prepared as a working paper of the Thesaurus Research Committee of the Deutsche Gesellschaft für Dokumentation by A Diemer, with categories 01 and 09 added. The gist of the proposal is that, although these categories may not be applicable in their entirety in every subject, they should always form the basis of facet construction within any subject, and the notation used should always be used consistently. As is pointed out in the discussion, these categories are of such general validity that even their first decimal division is likely to produce concepts of general rather than specific level, which will need further definition before they apply within any given subject field. (For example, one of the first steps of division of 02 would obviously lead to the concept ' parts '; this would have to be further defined in relation to a subject field such as, say, Engineering, before reaching the same level of specificity as the present hyphen auxiliaries for parts in 62.)

One is reminded of Ranganathan's seminal mnemonics,[66] the more so when one reads that the validity of these general categories is ' exclusively restricted to the idea plane '. While we may welcome the idea of consistency of notation throughout a scheme, there is no doubt that this implies that the notation will dictate the order; as it is a key principle that notation *must* be subsidiary, we should be cautious of any scheme that elevates it beyond this subsidiary role, no matter how attractive the proposition appears to be. Nevertheless, it is clear that development along the lines suggested would introduce a new level of consistency into the construction of UDC schedules which has already been sadly lacking in the past.

Class 0 was not used in the tabulation of new main classes, in order to reserve it for a kind of generalia class. This class would include a variety of concepts which can either form the object of study in themselves, or can form common facets applicable within the other main classes. The suggested tabulation is as follows:

01	Mathematical laws, natural laws, algorithms, formulae, concepts
02	inanimate matter; materials; minerals
03	plants
04	animals
05	persons
06	institutions, organizations
07	products (of technology)
08	documents
09	(spare)

The argument for including some of these headings is that we now need to be able to specify, for example, persons as persons rather than as the subjects of documents. This argument seems to be ill-founded; even with the current UDC it has always been possible to arrange—say —plants, as well as documents about plants, and this is true of almost any classification one cares to name. One may cite here the library of the Royal Botanic Gardens at Kew, where both the plant specimens and the documents about them are arranged by the taxonomic classification of Bentham and Hooker.[67] There *is* a need for general categories of the kind described, but they should be general and not in any way restrictive. The common subject subdivisions identified by the BNB are of this kind,[68] while the present UDC already has such facets for Persons and Materials, with Institutions forming part of the present Class o and also part of the Form common auxiliary. The latter is perhaps the best comparison, since Mrs Dahlberg proposes that the categories listed in her Class o should be used as subdivisions of the other main classes by means of a notational device; where at present we find 061 Associations in general 62(061) Associations relating to Engineering, we might in future find 62–061 used to express the same subject.

The existing .oo auxiliaries, the points-of-view numbers, are one of the major sources of confusion between common subdivisions and subdivisions specific to a particular subject. For example, it is difficult to justify both a Persons facet introduced by –05 *and* a Personnel point of view introduced by .007. Mrs Dahlberg suggests that a revised set of such subdivisions might be based on the general categories which are to form the basis of subdivisions within subject fields, and should then form a main class 001 to 009. From .07 Relations we would obtain

007 Relation as a general concept, and this would be the place where Perreault's system of relators would be included.

For syntagmatic organizations, Wellisch's bonding rule would be adopted; this would eliminate the need for any specified citation order, since the relationships between the various elements of a complex piece of notation would be indicated by their position. An example is quoted:

84.026.048.09   Evaluation of the redundancy of documentation systems

.09   .048   84   .026

The bonding rule shows precisely how this notation is to be interpreted. We may reorganize this example to illustrate the point further:

26.048.084.09   Evaluation of the documentation of system redundancy

or perhaps:

26.048.09.084   Documentation of the evaluation of systems **redundancy**. In each case the meaning is clear. (We are assuming here that main class numbers can be used as subdivisions in the way indicated, but this would appear to be the intention.)

This proposal is clearly a far-reaching one which deserves serious study. Some of its premises would appear to be debatable; for example, the proposed main class order seems to be open to as many objections as the present order. This does not detract from the overall value of the suggestions put forward, but merely that they will have to be examined in more detail before they can be accepted. However, there is no doubt that what is proposed is in fact *not* a revision of the present UDC but the compilation of a completely new scheme, which is a rather different matter. Revision of an existing scheme can be tolerated by users, as witness the fact that the ' phoenix ' schedules in DC (though the subject of bitter complaint when they appear) are adopted by libraries using the scheme.[69] It would be quite a different matter to expect users to start again from scratch with a scheme which appeared to be the same (through using the same notation) but was in fact quite different in every way. If the present UDC is to be abandoned in its entirety, there seems to be little point in discussing its future; the present author is not so pessimistic.

AN SRC FOR UNISIST

Midway between the minimum of revision and a complete supersession we have a kind of compromise solution; this involves restructuring the basic order while retaining detailed subdivision of particular topics very much as it stands at present. This idea is based on the proposition that what is needed for UNISIST is a relatively broad categorization, variously known as a Standard Reference Code or Standard Roof Classification, both of which conveniently abbreviate to SRC.[70] This broad classification should contain something of the order of 5,000 headings, and would be used as a 'switching' device, to enable users to get from one detailed indexing language to another. In practice, an abstracting service, for example, would carry a code (or codes) from the SRC to indicate its subject coverage in an internationally acceptable mode independent of language. The existence of such a code would, it is claimed, enable indexers in different countries to identify subject areas and the indexing languages appropriate to them. However, it is clear that such a limited code would not enable indexers to go any further towards identifying the detailed subject matter of particular documents; to make it possible for anyone to translate subject specifications from one indexing language into another, the intermediary switching code must be at least as detailed as either of the others, otherwise detail must inevitably be lost.[71] The purpose of the SRC as a switching code is therefore not clear, and it would appear that this aspect needs to be rethought. There would seem to be little point in developing a classification of this level of generality for this purpose.

If, however, we consider the SRC in relation to the revision of UDC a rather different pattern emerges, and one which might be of more value. As has already been pointed out, one major criticism of UDC is that its outline is based on that of DC, and is now outdated and anachronistic in many respects. Subjects which are relatively unimportant (from the documentation point of view), such as Philosophy, are given a single-digit notation, while others far more significant in today's terms, such as Nuclear Technology, have a base notation of six or more digits (621.039 in this instance). If it were possible to reallocate the notation for the major subject fields, it might still be feasible to use the existing detailed subdivisions very much as they stand. To explain this further, we may pursue the example of Nuclear Technology. The United Kingdom Atomic Energy Authority libraries normally abbreviate 621.039 to N for their own internal use: thus 621.039.524 becomes N.524. N is filed (arbitrarily) as if it were written out in its normal form. It should be clear that it would be possible to alter the significance of N without altering its subdivisions; N could now form part of the SRC, while one would continue to use UDC for detailed specification. In effect, this proposal would permit the long-awaited revision of the basic structure of UDC to take place while retaining all the detail which makes UDC attractive to many of its users. We may further make the point that, although this kind of change would require users to start a new sequence in their catalogues and on their shelves, such changes can be beneficial. Again citing the UKAEA, a new catalogue was started on January 1, 1959 to take advantage of new reprographic equipment which made it possible to produce standard 5″ × 3″ catalogue cards with all the detail used previously on 8″ × 5″ cards. Within a year, use made of the previous catalogue of report literature—one of the key tools for information retrieval in the UKAEA—had dropped to a very low level.[72] It may be argued that in a great many situations this is likely to be the pattern; even in the social sciences and humanities, where the emphasis on long term coverage within a single catalogue is almost a dogma, one may argue that, in fact, for the vast majority of users it is the most recent materials which are of interest and value.

Before waxing too enthusiastic over the SRC proposal, however, we should remember that it only tackles one part of the problem. We have already seen that there is a great deal of work to be done on revision of the detailed schedules as well as any overall restructuring. There would seem to be little point in putting the old wine of the full UDC schedules into the new SRC bottle, unless we believe enthusiastically that half a loaf is better than stale bread. There is also the point that the SRC would be open to just as much objection as the existing outline after a few years, unless steps were taken to keep it up to date. This brings us back to the fundamental point that any classification scheme is in effect an investment in obsolescence; once we start to use notation in a particular way, we shall be reluctant to alter our usage, because of the consequential work involved.

SECTION B : MANAGEMENT PROBLEMS

It is clear from many of the points discussed in chapter 3 that the key to the future development of UDC lies in changes in management rather than in changes in structure. So far, the present chapter has examined some of the changes that have been proposed in UDC structure, but in a forthright article Wellisch states flatly: ' in other words: the UDC suffers not so much from its hierarchical structure or its supposed backwardness, but rather from an almost complete lack of organization '.[73] The kind of system which worked reasonably well when the number of people engaged was small, and when one man at the centre could be expected to oversee development in its totality, cannot be expected to function well in a situation such as we have today. Many of the points made by Wellisch have already been discussed in chapter 3, but Wellisch takes the argument even further. He suggests that the present procedure for revision can, by virtue of its complexity, actually hinder real progress in revision. New schedules represent the needs of a minority, often an insignificant number of users; they become part of official UDC through publication as P-Notes and then as part of *Extensions and corrections,* when they are accepted and used only by the few who submitted them in the first place. Alternatively, they may be rejected at P-Note stage by the vote of one objector, who may not even be closely concerned. (Lloyd has used the term 'hyperdemocratic' to describe the procedure.) Furthermore, and perhaps more significantly, decisions on the validity of a change in the classification are taken by people who are not themselves experts in classification theory, or even in some cases closely concerned with the use of UDC. Present publication methods, particularly the lack of a current, complete, edition in English, form another severe barrier to the practical use of the scheme, which is not lessened by the practice of publishing P-Notes and *Extensions and corrections* in the language in which they are submitted: German, French or English, with occasional sections in other languages.

Wellisch proposes that major improvements in UDC can only come about as the result of a complete restructuring of the organization. Decision-making must be transferred from the Central Classification Committee to an editorial board consisting of four or five members working under a chief editor. The CCC would become a purely advisory body, and the present network of international and national subject committees would disappear, though the editors might well still consult subject experts throughout the world if the occasion arose. Revisions would be recorded on magnetic tape, which would be copied and distributed to national bodies, so that the latter could provide an instant information service on the current status of any particular section of the schedules. New editions of the full schedules, or rather the medium schedules which Wellisch believes to be more viable, would appear in the major languages English, German, French and Russian at regular intervals; every two or three years is suggested.

The proposals put forward for the revision of UDC, particularly those linked to the development of the SRC, have met with a considerable amount of opposition in Britain. The opposition has found a focus in the British National Committee, British Standards Institution Committee OC/20/4; after debating the effects of the proposed changes, the committee decided to hold an open meeting to alert British users at large to the threat to their present use of UDC, and this meeting was duly held on June 6, 1972, attracting nearly two hundred delegates. Most of those present were opposed to the development of a SRC, but this opposition seems to stem largely from two sources. We have already mentioned the inherent conservatism of any classification scheme; that librarians are reluctant to change because of the administrative work involved. This was certainly one source of opposition, but the other was, to some extent, a rather contrary point of view: that the diversion of funds to the production of the SRC would have a harmful effect on the already limited amount of revision work for UDC. Both of these matters are in fact aspects of the same facet of management: finance.

There is no doubt that the majority of the problems we have examined so far would not have arisen if sufficient funds had been available from the beginning to keep UDC revision and publication at an adequate level. Donker Duyvis may be said to have contributed to this problem by the very success with which he ran UDC for so many years; after his resignation, it was assumed that a similar organization (if one man with some secretarial help may be so described) would continue to suffice. This ignores the increase in the quantity of work to be done, but it also ignores the increase in the complexity of subjects occurring in documentation. It may be argued that the complexity explosion is more of a problem than the increase in quantity, since it requires a corresponding increase in sophistication of method rather than an expansion of existing methods. Publication of the English edition has taken thirty years because work on it has been carried on for most of that time at the same level: one man with a limited amount of secretarial help. It is only very recently that the amount of effort available in this country has been increased, as the result of a grant by the Office for Scientific and Technical Information to BSI to enable them to expand their activities in the field of documentation generally. In the light of the difficulties caused in the past by inadequate funding, it is a source of some concern that the amounts requested by the FID Classification Department appear to be far too small to provide the amount of effort required. The total subvention requested for 1972 is f20,000, about £2,600; the total estimated cost of preparing the SRC is put at about £2,200, spread over a period of years.[74] When one considers the 'competition' these sums appear ludicrous: the Decimal Classification Division employs about half a dozen people full-time on keeping the DC schedules up to date, while the Library of Congress has a much larger staff in its Subject Cataloguing Department. (It is not possible to estimate precisely the amount of effort devoted to the upkeep of LC schedules, because no distinction is made between classifying and classification development; the two activities are concomitant.) It also appears that because of the diversion of effort to the SRC, there has been some delay in the administrative processes relating to some schedule revisions which have been approved by the appropriate international committee.[75]

SOURCES OF FUNDS

If more money is to be spent, it must be found. Wellisch suggests that the sale of up-to-date, well-revised, medium editions would be sufficient to fund the development work necessary as well as the continuous revision which would still be involved, and instances DC as a successful project financially despite its deficiencies as a modern classification. It is certainly true that the English edition of UDC sells quite well, and one proposal that has been put forward as a counter to the suggested revisions of UDC is that BSI should in effect break away from FID and continue to publish the English edition as it stands, obtaining the money to finance this from sales. This would require a considerable increase in the amount of persuasion used to gain new users for the scheme, but a worth-while scheme, that is, one which is up-to-date and well presented, may well win over many who now consider UDC to be unsuitable for their purposes. The United States would present a more difficult market; there is little support for UDC there at present, despite the existence of a national committee with members such as Freeman and Rigby, but it may be that a vast untapped market exists. A great many information systems in the USA have developed their own thesauri, despite the existence of the EJC Thesaurus and similar largescale tools; evidently a need is felt for something beyond these tools, so why should not UDC serve this purpose? Despite the widespread use of the English edition, it would seem likely that without fairly considerable support from sales in the USA it would be difficult to finance the improvements which all agree to be necessary.

Other sources of funds exist, notably government agencies such as OSTI. OSTI is however not convinced of the value of UDC, and much work would have to be done to persuade them that they should provide largescale funds for its revision. One is faced with a chicken and egg situation: without funds, UDC cannot be radically improved, particularly in the short term, but an unimproved UDC is unlikely to attract funds.

Bodies such as the Council for Library Resources are unlikely to be willing to give funds to a project which would be of doubtful value in the USA. The National Science Foundation is probably too closely identified with other systems, such as the EJC Thesaurus, to agree to finance a 'rival' system, particularly in view of the reduction of US government funds available for research in library science generally. The work of Caless and his colleagues,[27] supported by the US Air Force Office of Scientific Research, came to an end before any conclusive results could be reached because it proved impossible to obtain funds for a further contract.

Despite the difficulties, funds must be found if UDC is not to die of inanition. The day of the enthusiastic amateur is past, nor is it proper that such an important scheme should have to rely on voluntary effort for its survival. A more realistic appraisal of these management problems in the past might well have avoided some of the most serious problems facing the scheme today.

SUMMARY

In this chapter some of the proposals which have been put forward recently for the more or less complete revision of UDC have been examined. Some are seen to be less than convincing in that the solutions they propose do not appear to offer a sufficient improvement over the present scheme to make their implementation worthwhile; others are seen to be worthwhile, but to require finance which at present is not available. In general, one may say that if the necessary improvements could be made in the managerial structure, as suggested by Wellisch, then improvements in the structure of the schedules could be expected to follow as a natural consequence. To try to improve the classification without giving first priority to management reorganization would lead to little or no change for the better, and might indeed lead, through the dissipation of resources, to a deterioration of the position. A revised, rationalized and easily available UDC could fill a need which certainly exists.

CHAPTER 5

MECHANIZATION AND UDC

One of the first attempts to mechanize an index classified by UDC was probably that carried out at the library of the Atomic Energy Research Establishment, Harwell.[76] This used punched cards, not a computer, but some of the conclusions are nevertheless of relevance to any mechanized system.

The index constructed was in two parts: one of these was the file of punched cards, the other a card index filed by report serial number. The punched cards were used in fixed field mode, with five fields of sixteen columns into which UDC numbers were punched; additionally the report serial number and title were typed on. A search might involve running the pack of cards, which reached some 6,500 after two years, through the machine four times to search the appropriate fields (the fifth field being used only for the common auxiliaries of language, form and place). The machine was not particularly powerful, being capable of searching up to eight columns simultaneously. A search would reveal a set of cards; reference had then to be made to the visual index via the report number to find out whether the report was likely to be relevant or not.

Problems arose in a variety of ways; the one which perhaps contributed most to the decision to go over to a conventional visual index was wear and tear on the cards, which would not occur in a computer system, but two of the intellectual problems are more serious. The first of these was the inability to modify a search while it was being actually carried out. The possibility of conducting heuristic searches (*ie* searches which can be modified *at the time* in the light of information found in the course of searching) is one of the most valuable features of the conventional card catalogue, and recent research with computerized systems such as MEDLARS[77] has emphasized the importance of ' interactive ' searching as opposed to iterative. Any system devised for use with UDC in the future will have to have on-line searching capabilities if it is to be really worthwhile. The second was the problem of setting the search level: if too narrow a search was conducted, it might well reject relevant material with slightly different class numbers, whereas too broad a search would lead to the low relevance factor always associated with high recall—the enquirer would be faced with a mass of material which he would have to look through by hand. For example, a document on a particular linear particle accelerator might be classified at 621.384.644 Particle accelerators—linear—using waveguides; a search which specified the type of waveguide, *eg* corrugated, will not reveal this document because the UDC number will be too specific: 621.384.644.3. On the other hand, a search for ' linear accelerators ' 621.384.64 will reveal material on accelerators using waveguides, certainly, but also those using drift tubes, plasma or any other means of acceleration. In any system using UDC, or indeed any classification scheme involving notation, setting the right search level can cause difficulties; here again an interactive system, where the user gets an instantaneous, or at least a rapid, response, can save time in searching.

A third point, which concerns the classifier, was the fact that past indexing practice was not conveniently displayed. In any system, a set of indexing habits will grow up; a document will be classified in a particular way because similar documents have been treated in that way in the past. If the classifier cannot easily consult past practice, such aids to consistency are not available, not to mention the additional work involved in re-making decisions.

The difficulties experienced at Harwell and in similar experiments led to something of a moratorium on the use of mechanized systems for UDC, but in 1960 Rigby started to use a computer in the production and indexing of *Meteorological and geoastrophysical abstracts*.[38] This service has been classified by UDC since 1949, but no attempt was made to introduce mechanization until it was felt that the available machines and programs would be worth using. It is interesting to note that Rigby gives as one of the reasons for the delay that:

> 'Available experience, both within our organization, and in the service bureaus, was insufficient to provide the intellectual input for designing a durable system '.

We can probably claim to have overcome most machine limitations by now, but intellectual problems still remain to be solved whenever we attempt to set up a new retrieval system.

The UDC parts of Rigby's work covered several distinct aspects. The first of these was the preparation of Authority lists showing past classificatory practice. Two printouts were made, one arranged alphabetically, the other by UDC number. From there it proved to be possible to work out cross-reference networks, eliminate synonyms, identify UDC sections in need of expansion, and provide verbal extensions to non-specific UDC numbers where necessary.[78] Another important part of the work was the indexing and arrangement of bibliographies by UDC, including *Meteorological and geoastrophysical titles;* the programs developed also made it possible to print out other indexes, *eg* alphabetical subject or journals covered. It was also shown that preparation and updating of UDC schedules was perfectly feasible; during the ten or so years since this work was carried out, FID have gone so far as to introduce the use of a punched tape typewriter with a view to future computerization of the schedules and their publication, but one can hardly regard this as a serious response.[79] Rigby has been one of the most enthusiastic supporters of UDC in the United States, and his recent contribution to the University of Maryland School of Library and Information Services Symposium[80] is a useful summary of the problems.

FREEMAN AND ATHERTON

Perhaps the largest-scale project to investigate the use of UDC in mechanized systems has been that sponsored by the American Institute of Physics and carried out by R R Freeman and Mrs P Atherton.[81] Freeman had been involved with Rigby's work, and published an important paper in 1964[82] on computers and classification systems. The AIP was looking for a classification system to use to organize the literature of physics (AIP publishes a substantial part of the significant English-language journal literature in this field) and UDC seemed a potential candidate. A grant was secured from the National Science Foundation—the sum involved was $200,000—and the work began with a study of the current state of the art of mechanized retrieval systems. Work on UDC for the project fell into three basic parts: convert UDC to machine-readable form; run an information retrieval system using UDC; obtain experimental user evaluation of the results. Put like this, the project seems reasonably simple; hardly worth $200,000. In practice, a number of problems were encountered. The first of these, the difficulty of obtaining the schedules in order to convert them, has been mentioned briefly in chapter 3. At the time, work on the full

528 GEODESY AND SURVEYING
528.4 FIELD- AND LAND SURVEYING
528.9 CARTOGRAPHY. MAPPING. *Cf. 912*

53 Physics and mechanics

53.01 **THEORY. NATURE OF SPECIFIC PHENOMENA** *Cf. 530.1*
53.07 **EQUIPMENT. APPARATUS. MODELS, ETC.**
53.08 **MEASUREMENT: PRINCIPLES, METHODS.** *Cf. 681.2*
53.081 **UNITS. CONSTANTS**
53.082 **PRINCIPLES OF MEASUREMENT AND INSTRUMENTS**
53.082.16 Gyroscopic instruments
53.082.2/.6 Various p incip es *Subdivide as 532/536*
53.082.7 **Use of electrical, magnetic and nuclear phenomena**
53.082.74 Electromagnetic and electrodynamic phenomena
53.082.76 Perturbation phenomena
53.082.79 Nuclear phenomena
53.083 **METHODS OF MEASUREMENT. DIRECT. RESONANCE, BALLISTIC, ZERO METHODS, ETC.**
53.084 **CONSTRUCTION OF INSTRUMENTS. COMPONENTS**
53.084.82/.89 Storage and transmission of matter and energy in various forms . *Broadly as 532/539, e.g. 53.084.89 Radioactive substances, ionized substances*.
53.085 **READING DEVICES: INDICATORS, POINTERS, ETC. SCALES, VERNIERS, DIALS, ETC.**
53.087 **OBSERVATION. RECORDING**
53.087.2/.3 Subjective observation
53.087.4 Objective observation in general
53.087.5 Photographic recording
53.087.6 Graphic recording
53.087.9 Devices for computing, printing, etc.
53.088 **ACCURACY. ERRORS. CORRECTIONS. CHECKING**
53.089 **CALIBRATION, ETC.**
530.1 **GENERAL PRINCIPLES OF PHYSICS. GENERAL THEORY OF FIELDS AND TRANFORMATIONS. (INVARIANCE PRINCIPLE)**

532 **FLUID MECHANICS** *Class here material relating to the mechanics of both liquids and gases*
532.1 **HYDROSTATICS**
532.12 **Compressibility**
532.13 **Viscosity . Fluidity**
532.135 Non-Newtonian viscosity . Non-Newtonian fluids . **Rheology**
532.137 Measurement of viscosity . Viscometers
532.21 **Surface level of liquids**
532.217 Measurement and control of liquid level . Indicators . Instruments for automatic control of level and for interface control
532.217.084.89 Liquid level indicators using radiation sources (including isotopes) *Cf. 621.039.84*
532.5 **FLUID DYNAMICS**
532.5.011.12 Reynolds number
532.51 **Motion of fluids . Fluid flow**
532.517 Flow in viscous fluids
532.517.2 Laminar flow . Streamline flow
532.517.4 Turbulence . Turbulent flow . *Cf. 532.542.4*
532.522 Flow through nozzels, orifices and jets *Cf. 621.647.3*
532.526 Flow at boundary layer . Skin friction
532.527 Vortices . Rotational flow
532.528 Cavitation . *Cf. 620.193.16*
532.529 Flow in gas-liquid mixtures . Motion of gases in liquids
532.529.3 Diffusion of a jet in surrounding liquid
532.529.6 Motion of gas bubbles and liquid drops . Bubble formation
532.542 Flow in pipes and tubes
532.542.4 Turbulent flow in pipes and tubes
532.546 Flow through porous media . Percolation processes
532.57 **Measurement of quantity and rate of flow**
532.57.08 Flowmeters in general
532.57.082.74 Electromagnetic flowmeters
532.58 **Hydrodynamics of submerged or floating bodies in a moving fluid . Drag . Resistance to motion**
532.584 Fluid-solid suspension
532.59 Wave motion . Waves
532.595.2 Pressure surges in pipes . Explosion waves in liquids . Theory of water hammer

Figure 1   Computer-produced UDC schedules

528.5 **Geodetic instruments and equipment.** *Cf.* 531.7
.51 Distance and length measuring equipment
.52 Angle and direction: theodolites, etc.
.53 Combined: tacheometers, plane tables, etc.
.54 Height, depth, inclination measuring: levels

528.7 PHOTOGRAMMETRY
Photographic details, *see* 77, 778.3
.71 Aerial and terrestrial techniques
.72 Orientation and restitution of photograms
.73 Aerial triangulation

528.9 CARTOGRAPHY. MAPPING. *Cf.* 912
.91 Theory, principles: scale, marginal data

528.92 Practical map design, drawing, reproduction
.93 Topographical and landscape representation.
.94/.95 Thematic cartography. Globe and relief

529 CHRONOLOGY. Time. **The calendar**
.1 Day. Sidereal day. Solar day
.2 Time calculation in general
.3 Calendars in general. Perpetual calendar
.4 Christian calendar
.5 Calendar reform
.7 Time measurement. *Cf.* 389.2; 522.5; 531.76
.78 Apparatus and instruments: sundials, gnomons

53 Physics and Mechanics

53.01 Theory, nature of specific phenomena. *Cf.* 530.1
53.07 Equipment, apparatus, models, etc.
53.08 **Measurement: principles, methods.** *Cf.* 681.2
.081 Units. Constants
.082 Principles of measurement and instruments
.16 Gyroscopic instruments
.2/.7 Various principles. *As* 532/537
.083 Methods of measurement. Direct, resonance, ballistic, zero methods, etc.
.084 Construction of instruments. Components.
.085 Reading devices; indicators, pointers, etc.
Scales, verniers, dials, etc.
.087 Observation. Recording
.2/.3 Subjective observation
.4 Objective observation in general

531.4 **Work. Friction**
.41 Work. Efficiency
.42 Weight, mass, specific gravity, density
   Cf. 531.21; 531.75
.43 Friction in general. *Cf.* 539.62
.44 Sliding or slipping friction
.45 Rolling friction
.46 Combined slipping and rolling friction

531.5 **Gravitation. Ballistics**
.51 Gravitation. Gravity. *Cf.* 528.27; 531.26
.52 Laws of falling bodies
.53 Pendulum theory, laws
.55 External ballistics. Motion of projectiles
.56 Secondary motion of projectiles in the air.

Figure 2   Comparable schedules from the abridged English edition

English edition had not progressed very far; of the 103 sections listed, only thirty two were easily available, and sixteen of these were accounted for by the major sections published in 1943: Generalities, Auxiliaries, and Science.[83] The abridged edition was of course available and was the first to be converted to machine-readable form. The manuscript of the German medium edition was used as the basis for expanding this, involving a considerable translation effort. Eventually, all the available schedules were transferred via paper tape to magnetic tape, sorted and listed, giving a total of some 100,000 entries. It was thought that the degree of overlap resulting from the methods used would lead to a reduction of this figure to a ' true ' level of about 70,000 headings, somewhat larger than the medium edition level. As a side-issue, programs were developed to print out the schedules from this input, using the length of the UDC number as a guide to type face, indentation etc. As UDC notation is not always expressive, this could lead to unsatisfactory results, but the results obtained were quite impressive (*figure 1*). It is interesting to compare the results with the schedules as they appear in the abridged edition (*figure 2*); such a comparison suggests that the mechanical approach loses little in the majority of situations. The printing was done by filmsetting, the work being carried out by an outside contractor, Inforonics Inc, and was somewhat expensive; if COM were to be used, present-day costs might well be surprisingly acceptable compared with normal printed editions.[84] The experience gained in classification management as a result of this part of the project has been published by Freeman[85] in a valuable contribution to classification technology.

The survey conducted by Freeman and Atherton, together with a number of papers at the 1965 FID Conference in Washington,[86] had shown that IBM had already developed a potentially useful set of programs, the Combined File Search System.[87] This had only been used for alphabetical systems up to that time, but there seemed to be no reason why it should not be valid for UDC searching, and this proved to be the case. There were certain features which were particularly attractive, three of these being selected by Freeman for special mention.[88] First we may select the facility for generic searching pinpointed by the AERE experience; with CFSS, one can select a word stem and find all the occurrences of that stem no matter what follows, and it proved to be simple to use this facility with UDC. To quote the example demonstrated earlier, we can search with equal ease for 621.384.64, 621.384.644, or 621.384.644.3; if we search for 621.384.644 we shall find all its subdivisions as well. This does not in itself give us any very great advantage over punched cards, except in the ease with which the operation can be conducted and the far greater speed, but combined with the second feature it can be a great step forward. This is the ability to search for 'sub-descriptors'; descriptors which only have meaning when associated with a main heading. This describes the special auxiliaries in UDC precisely, and also the point of view numbers: —, .o and .oo have no meaning unless attached to a main UDC number. (These are Wellisch's non-detachable auxiliaries; the connectives which go to make up Wellisch's complete set—colon, stroke, etc—were not encoded in the AIP experiments.) Using these two facilities it would be possible to frame a search to find anything on Fractional distillation in Chemical technology as 66xxx.048.3, where xxx can be any set of digits. (But note that this would *not* reveal Fractional distillation of Petroleum, which is enumerated at 665.52!) The third facility is that of linking descriptors to avoid false drops in a situation where a document deals with more than one subject. For example, we may consider the Symposium referred to in [79] and [80]; this contains papers on 'The UDC in mechanized subject information retrieval' and 'Library of Congress subject headings—review and forecast'. The use of links would prevent the retrieval of this document in response to a search for 'Library of Congress subject headings in mechanized subject information retrieval', and this feature is thus a valuable one.

CFSS also permits the use of logical operators: AND, OR and NOT. This is a facility which does not exist in the same way in manual systems, where searches involving this kind of logic have to be carried out serially. For example, if we wished to conduct a search in a manual index for anything on 'beam guiding devices in particle accelerators other than electromagnets' it would be feasible but extremely tedious; the amount of work involved in scanning selectively would almost certainly lead to human error.[89] Using CFSS it is possible to search for 621.384.6xxx15 AND NOT 621.318.3; this kind of search can be performed quickly and accurately by the computer, and this is in fact a standard facility with most programs of this type.

Problems with UDC notation have already been mentioned briefly in chapter 3, and some details can now be examined. They are summarized by Freeman as follows:

(1) Some of the notational devices of UDC serve the function of visual convenience; this function is meaningless in a computer.

(2) Some of the notational devices use the same punctuation symbols. The order of sorting these symbols, arbitrarily defined for each type of computer, causes some problems when they are interspersed among digits in UDC numbers, especially if the user desires to adhere to UDC filing rules.

(3) Some of the notational devices require recognition of two characters in order to differentiate between devices. For example, the equals sign has one meaning by itself and another if it is preceded by a parenthesis.

(4) Two of the devices (.o and .oo) incorporate a meaningful use of what is otherwise a convenience symbol, the decimal point.

To enlarge a little on some of these points, (1) refers to the point, used in UDC to break up lengthy pieces of notation into convenient three-digit sets; there is no point (if we may so express it) in doing this in a computer system. (2) relates to a serious problem which is still being investigated: the question of filing rules for entries in mechanized systems.[90] The use of arbitrary symbols as facet indicators in UDC may be regarded as an advantage in manual systems,[91] because it enables the classifier to change the citation order *and* the filing order at the same time, and thus retain the advantages of inversion while gaining the advantages of a citation order more suited to his needs. This kind of manipulation is not necessary in a computer system; what *is* essential is a standardized filing order which can be recognized without special programming by the computer. (3) is shown to the greatest extent by the parenthesis; it means one thing if followed by o [form division], another if followed by a digit from 1 to 9 [place division], and a third if followed by = [race and nationality division]. This would require a subroutine to be called in whenever the computer recognized an opening parenthesis, and though this would be perfectly feasible it did not form part of the existing CFSS package. Similar considerations apply to (4). It was therefore decided to replace all the facet indicators by letters to give the standard UDC filing order as set out in the abridged English edition; thus (o became F, (1/9 became PI/9 and (= became R. Main numbers were preceded by c, and decimal points were omitted; thus 621.384.644.3 became c6213846443 —not at all convenient for manual use but perfectly satisfactory for the computer.

The system could be used in both batch and on-line mode, and one of the reports on the project is devoted to AUDACIOUS—AUtomatic Direct ACcess to Information with the on-line Udc system.[92] Few systems of this kind had been developed at the time, though some experimental work had been carried out, and it was decided to use a system designed by the Information Systems Division of Xerox Corporation to retrieve information relating to doctoral dissertations, DATRIX. Additional features were built in to enable the user to prepare his search strategy. The basic UDC schedules were those of the *Special subject edition for nuclear science and technology*[34]; these formed one file. A separate file consisted of references from one issue of *Nuclear science abstracts*, classified by members of the UKAEA using the UDC schedules (which are based on UKAEA practice). To determine which UDC numbers he wished to search, the user typed in at a console the words he first thought of; provided that these words were used in the UDC schedules, the corresponding UDC numbers would be displayed on the screen of the console. To obtain a display of related class numbers, the user could type in another command, indicating which class number he wished to use as the basis of the display; the computer would then cause the hierarchy at that point to appear on the screen. Another instruction enabled the user to obtain a display of instructions telling him how to use the system.

Once the appropriate UDC numbers had been established, the user could link them by logical operators if necessary and then instruct the computer to search the document file; references found to match the search strategy would then be displayed on the screen. Alternatively the user could ask first for a count of the references satisfying the search, and thus avoid overenthusiastic recall by restating his search strategy if necessary.

Considering that this was the first attempt to use UDC in such a system, with data not specially prepared and users unaccustomed to either UDC or the system, results were very good. Many of the objections arose out of unfamiliarity; others stemmed from the fact that insufficient time and money could be devoted to adaptations of the program that would have led to greatly increased user satisfaction. Users were not discouraged by some of the factors which have often been advanced as disadvantages of computer systems, for example a limitation to upper case letters only; much more serious was the need for users to perform fairly complicated typing sequences at the console in order to operate the system at all, a problem which is relatively simple to overcome.

In their conclusions, Freeman and Atherton point out the value of a notated system, such as UDC, for international exchange networks where the problem of language might otherwise prove a serious barrier. They also suggest the use of UDC in conjunction with a thesaurus; an authority file, that is, very similar to *Thesaurofacet*. Perhaps the most significant conclusion for the librarian is that:

' For system designers, clearly, the most important implication of the results of AUDACIOUS is the need for careful consideration of the user viewpoint in all facets of the design of an interactive retrieval system. A system which is a technical success can fail to impress an information system user ...'

There is no doubt that AUDACIOUS and the rest of the AIP project showed without any doubt at all that UDC was satisfactory for use in mechanized systems, and that it was perfectly feasible to produce UDC schedules by computer-controlled typesetting. Yet none of this work has been utilized in practical terms in this country, a situation which seems almost incredible. No use has been made of the ' medium edition ' produced as a by-product and available on magnetic tape and on microfiche; certainly some editing would be needed before it could be accepted as fully satisfactory in conventional terms, but if we consider the unsound basis for any abridgement, discussed in chapter 2, it remains a matter for wonder that this work has been ignored. The reason advanced is that all available effort had to be concentrated on completing the full edition; any effort devoted to the production of a medium edition from the AIP working version would have postponed that objective yet further. However, Wellisch[73] is firmly of the opinion that the medium (' pocket ') edition is what is really required; he sees little need for the full edition, particularly in the light of the synthetic nature of UDC:

' The present UDC in a size approximately equal to the German pocket edition can meet almost all the requirements of an inter-national ' switching language ', provided that two conditions are met: a) a thorough ' cleaning up ' of the main numbers ... b) the system of auxiliary numbers itself must be revised, improved, extended and generalized ...'

There would be no point in stopping work on the English full edition at this point, with only a few fascicules left to complete it (subject to the need for extensive updating and revision), but in 1967 the position was very different, and it seems more than likely that the British National Committee came to the wrong decision when it chose to put the AIP work on one side.[93]

In the event, the British were not the only people to put the work on one side. The AIP itself decided not to pursue the matter further, but to develop instead a rather simple faceted classification scheme for their own purposes. Despite the enthusiasm and good work of such workers as Rigby and Freeman and Atherton, little progress can be recorded in furthering the acceptance of UDC in the United States, though the author's own experience shows that students who are introduced to UDC at library school in the USA are very impressed by it and puzzled by its lack of popularity. The AIP project seems to have roused most interest in Europe, and the FID has now held three seminars on UDC in mechanized information retrieval systems[94]; the first of these was largely devoted to the AIP project, but the second and third have contained papers from a variety of sources, showing the widespread interest that exists, at least on this side of the Atlantic.

AMERICAN GEOLOGICAL INSTITUTE

The American Geological Institute produces the monthly *Bulletin and abstracts of geological literature excluding North America;* each abstract contains a UDC number, but the annual subject index is an alphabetical one. In 1968 the institute commissioned a private company, Infodata Systems Inc, to investigate the possibilities of mechanizing the service, using a set of programs entitled INQUIRE somewhat similar to the Xerox Corporation system used by Freeman and Atherton. The system was keyed to the verbal descriptors of the annual index, but it was possible to search the text of each abstract for character strings. The file contained about 11,000 abstracts for each year, and a sequential search through all of these, character by character, took ten minutes; a search by keyword, or year of publication, narrowed this down—in the case of keywords to a few seconds. Despite the fact that the system was not in any way geared to the UDC codings, it proved to be possible to perform quite sophisticated searches; if the search could first be narrowed down by selecting an appropriate keyword, search times were negligible. What was particularly interesting was that by using the UDC numbers it proved to be possible to carry out searches which would have been impossible using only the keywords. On Christmas Eve 1965 a large meteorite fell near the Leicestershire village of Barwell; its size can be gauged from the fact that a report in *Nature* noted that over fifty kilograms of fragments had been collected by mid-1966. A search in the keyword index under Barwell

79

would have been successful, but a search under Leicestershire would not; the indexing was only under specific place names. A search for (452.42 would however have retrieved this and any other information about Leicestershire with no difficulty at all. The power of conducting generic searches by using UDC numbers was well shown by this system, and another typical search is shown in Appendix C. There is no doubt that commercially available on-line retrieval systems such as this can use UDC quite successfully; they may not have all the refinements that one could wish for, but this is mainly because of problems arising from the unsatisfactory nature of the UDC schedules, not from computer problems.

CALESS

The work of Caless and his colleagues has already been referred to,[27] but some aspects deserve rather fuller treatment. Caless has been more concerned with the refinements that would make UDC a really powerful indexing language for machine searching, and has put forward one or two ideas which have not been explored elsewhere. The work began at the VELA Seismic Information Analysis Center of the University of Michigan, where the steady growth of the report collection beyond 10,000 documents (not perhaps a figure at which British librarians would have felt a need to mechanize) had led to serious consideration of machine retrieval systems. The first task was to revise the UDC Seismology schedules at 550.34, which was done by Mills, the P-Note being issued in 1966. At the same time, the staff of the Center were trained in the use of UDC. The method used to build up the input was the analysis mentioned briefly in chapter 4; any UDC string can be expressed in the form $M_1S_1S_2S_3M_2S_4S_5S_6M_3S_7S_8M_4S_9$ etc, where M represents a main number, S an auxiliary. Relationships can now be tabulated:

M_1S_1	M_2S_4	M_3S_7	M_4S_9
M_1S_2	M_2S_5	M_3S_8	S_7S_8
M_1S_3	M_2S_6	S_5S_6	S_4S_6
S_1S_2	S_2S_3	S_1S_3	S_4S_5 etc

If the sense is taken into account, many of the combinations given by a mechanical approach to this analysis can be eliminated without loss. Those that remain are entered into the system, with a field code to show the relationship; eg a .o auxiliary attached to a main number is given field code 28, a (...) auxiliary (ie place or form) is given field code 43. The auxiliary notation does not, of course, have to be entered, nor, in this particular case, was it necessary to enter 550.34, which formed part of every class number. Searches could use Boolean operators AND, OR and NOT, but also the logical operators GREATER THAN, EQUAL and LESS THAN: this enables the connective symbols / and +, lost entirely in the AIP work, to be effectively replaced.

To obtain the required analysis Caless suggested the use of matrices[95] which have a strong family resemblance to Ranganathan's *rounds* but use such headings as Operations, Agents, Parts etc rather than PMEST. The use of such a matrix certainly helps the classifier faced with a typical subject such as that quoted by Caless.

Shallow depth earthquakes related to California aftershock sequences of short duration.

for which the suggested UDC number is:

550.348.436.098.23 : 550.384.433(*AFTER)(794)"403"

The matrix will also be of considerable help in constructing the necessary alphabetical index entries. If we consider the matrix headings as role indicators, we find a resemblance also to a PRECIS statement of the subject; the suggested headings for Science and Technology are as follows; PRECIS operators, discussed in chapter 6, are shown for each:

Whole thing(4) or (6)

Kinds	/ or ,
Parts	(p)
Materials	(p)
Processes	(3)
Properties	(q)
Operations	(3)
Agents	(2)

It will be seen that the order of application does not clash with the PRECIS operators, remembering that (p) and (q) can be introduced wherever appropriate. There is a slight difference from PMEST in that Properties are now regarded as (M) and would thus precede Processes, which, like Operations, form part of (E).

The bonding proposals put forward by Perreault and Wellisch both use square brackets to enclose conceptual units and show order of precedence of the notational symbols used as indicators. Caless has put forward an alternative, the use of Polish notation,[96] which may have certain advantages for computer manipulation. An expression in Polish notation consists of a binary operator and two operands, which can either be simple operands or another Polish expression. A UDC number can be converted into a string of operators and operands which automatically indicates which parts belong to which without the need for specific grouping devices such as square brackets. Operands may be labelled as Left L or Right R, so that an expression may be written as L operator R; for Polish notation, the operator is moved to the left of the two operands, so that the string is filed in the computer as O L R, such a string itself serving as a Left or Right operand if necessary. To demonstrate, we may take a pair of examples quoted by Wellisch to clarify the effect of square brackets: [52]

75.023.2:[667.6:669.71]   Manufacture of aluminium paint for artists' paints

[75.023.2:667.6]:669.71   Aluminium for the manufacture of artists' paints

Using Polish notation these would be coded as follows; operands are shown as L or R for clarity:

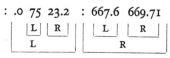

and:

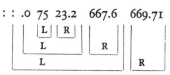

The difference between the bonding precedences is thus shown by the form of the string. Polish notation is already used as a convenient stringing device, used in list processing in computers, and its application to UDC could give interesting results.

To search for a particular string of notation, it is only necessary to code the search in the same way; for example, to search for aluminium paint 667.6:669.71 we would code the search as O L R:

:667.6 669.71

It will be seen that such a search would reveal the first document demonstrated above, but not the second, since the string we require does not appear in the coding for the latter.

OTHER WORK

There has of course been a great deal of other work on the use of UDC in mechanized systems which will not be examined here. UDC has shown itself satisfactory in the production of indexing services such as

Documentatio geographica,[97] in the maintenance of library catalogues[98] and in the provision of SDI services.[99] Much of this work has been described in the three seminars organized by the FID[94] or is well documented in the published literature, and there is no point in rehearsing these well-proven arguments. It is clear that despite many problems UDC can be used now with good results in the stringent conditions imposed by mechanized systems. Certainly no more than this can be said even of those systems specially designed with mechanization in mind, since they operate under the same constraints of indexer consistency, recall and precision. It would appear that the potential of UDC in this area is such that effort should be devoted to its improvement where necessary rather than dissipated in the construction of a multitude of new indexing languages.

SUMMARY

This chapter has set out to show that the use of UDC in mechanized systems is feasible and that many of the problems, such as the lack of adequate schedules, are trivial in that they can be cured relatively easily; no fundamental problems have been found. UDC schedules can themselves be maintained by mechanized methods, which could solve the problem of lack of convenient method of updating existing schedules and publishing new ones. The possibility of using sophisticated indexing techniques is exciting, particularly if machine searching means that devices intended to increase precision can be ignored very easily if high recall is required. We are forced again to the conclusion that the major problems facing UDC are not those of content (though these must not be discounted) but those of management; mechanization could provide a solution.

CHAPTER 6

THE WORK OF THE CRG: TOWARDS A NEW GENERAL CLASSIFICATION SCHEME

The history of the CRG has been demonstrated by D J Foskett, Crossley and Wilson,[100] and there is no need to repeat it here. As was pointed out in chapter 1, by the end of the first decade of their work, the CRG members felt able to compile a satisfactory classification ' on demand ' for any given subject area which could be defined as reasonably homogeneous. The technique can now be used as a teaching method, and has proved successful at the University of Maryland School of Library and Information Services and at the College of Librarianship Wales.[101] It became increasingly clear, however, that to compile separate classification schemes for each and every occasion was a relatively inefficient procedure, for the reasons stated: the recurrence of certain facets; and coverage of fringe topics. The CRG therefore bent its thoughts towards the construction of a new general classification, and succeeded in obtaining a grant of £5,000 from NATO to pay some of the costs. A conference was held in 1963 to set the scene and outline the problems,[102] and work then began on the necessary preliminaries. A series of thirteen reports were prepared by the two research assistants involved, and have been published in a convenient single volume;[103] we can examine the ideas put forward and trace their development to the point where the grant ran out. This volume does not however include the report in which Austin first introduced the idea of general systems theory; this long paper would have helped to give a basic unifying theme to his other contributions.[103a]

LEVELS OF INTEGRATION

One of the theories investigated was the theory of integrative levels: the idea that the whole is more than the sum of its parts because it also involves *organization*. To follow through an example: one may take a collection of parts made of steel and other similar metals, but they do not form a piston until they are assembled in a particular way; one can then take several pistons, various other parts, and assemble them, but until they are assembled they cannot give power; an engine on its own, together with all the rest of the necessary parts, does not make a car. At each level the parts are brought together in an organized way to form a new entity, a new level of integration. The theory has been put forward by several writers in relation to library classification, notably by D J Foskett,[104] but the CRG found that it was of only limited value. Difficulties arose in two ways: different chains of integration, and problems of aggregation.

Starting with fundamental particles, one can build up a series of integrative levels, through nuclei, atoms and molecules, but at this point the chain branches, to take different directions for living and non-living substances. At the present we are not able to integrate further, because we do not know the essential difference between life and non-life. A similar dichotomy must arise at present if we reach the level ' man '; in one direction we have a series of social integrations, in another a series of intellectual integrations. The CRG work has not in fact included any detailed study of ' mentefacts ',[105] but did include the application of levels of integration to several subject areas, including biology, geology and mining, astronomy and physics. The theory was found to be of value, but not by any means overwhelming in its power.

The second problem, that of levels of aggregation, leads to further confusion. The difference is best illustrated by the distinction normally made between a compound and a mixture: in the former, the intrinsic characteristics of the original components can no longer be detected, whereas in the latter they are still recognizable. For example, we may separate the iron from a mixture of iron filings and sulphur by using a magnet, but once the two ingredients have formed a compound, for example by heating them together, a magnet has no effect; the iron is no longer present *as iron*. Similarly, if we examine social structures, for example, we find that the components of a family retain their individualities, and the family itself remains recognizably the same unit even with the passage of time. It would seem that the levels of complexity shown by aggregates differ from those of integrated systems, even though aggregates are always formed from entities belonging to particular integrative levels. For example, having reached ' man ' as an integrative level, we can then see him in various aggregates: family, committee, school class, community, etc.

A further question which presents itself is that of *dis*integration. Here again we see a fundamental difference between living and non-living entities, in that there is no equivalent of ' death ' for the latter. It is suggested that a notational symbol might be used to ' distinguish pork from pig, lumber from tree, perhaps morphology from physiology '. However, it is a little difficult to see how such a device would lead to any kind of useful order among what might be termed the products of death, since uses after death do not always parallel relationships in life. Disaggregation leads to similar problems, which may vary from aggregate to aggregate:

' ... the row
' that broke up our society upon the Stanislow '
left the members of that society more or less intact,[106] but the sands of the shore did not form part of the process which led to the aggregate from which they themselves are formed.

The ideas associated with the theory of integrative levels can be of value in the analysis of subjects for the construction of a classification scheme, but it would seem that they must be used within their limitations; other ideas are likely to prove more generally useful.

CATEGORIES

The idea of grouping concepts into categories according to some common factor is basic to the whole process of facet analysis, and a large part of the CRG work was devoted to the investigation of this approach. Ranganathan's *Fundamental categories* are useful as a starting point, but their limitation to three (four in CC7), even when expanded by the use of rounds and levels, means that their generality renders them rather weak in analysis. A rather more detailed list of categories was drawn up, as follows:

Entity
Stage
Part
Constituent
Properties
Self-activities
Actions affecting other entities
Acted on by other entities

Method of study

Tool

These categories were investigated in relation to mining, geology, sculpture, physics and politics, with some success. A further general category was proposed, that of ' systems ', which later took on a more significant role. There was also felt to be a need for some means of representing ' pathology ', corresponding to some extent to Ranganathan's seminal mnemonic 4; ' hazards ' in mining did not seem to fit well into any of the proposed categories, yet in many instances a hazard is merely the result of a *malfunction* in an already classified concept. However, a problem that was seen here was the one which we have already mentioned in commenting on Dahlberg's proposed main classes: the locations of such concepts as parasitism depends on the point of view, and a concept which might fall into the ' malfunction ' category from one point of view might well not do so if viewed from a different standpoint. Radioactive disintegration is a perfectly normal phenomenon, indeed, it is one which cannot be prevented, but it leads to the eventual disappearance of the source element.

CONSECUTIVENESS

The examination of the results of applying the theory of integrative levels to naturally occurring entities led to a further important idea: that of time-dependence, denoted ' consecutiveness ' by Austin. Levels of integration form a branching pattern, as we have seen; to fit them into the essentially linear sequence of a documentary classification scheme it is necessary to impose some further constraint. Austin found that in many cases ' time of emergence ' formed just such a constraint as was required. Thus the products of disintegration would follow their source in the sequence, though they might well be at a lower level of integration; similarly artefacts would follow their source. This idea links up with a similar concept, that of ' drives ' or purpose. Feibleman's fifth law states: for an organization at any given level, its mechanism lies at the level below, and its purpose at the level above.[107] It is perhaps worth noting here that both of these ideas are contrary to the principle of reductionism, which suggests that in order to understand an organization we need only break it down into its fundamental constituent parts; to do this implies that we must ignore purpose and time sequence.

It was at this point that Austin introduced the idea of systems theory, that is, 'those relationships which unite things into systems in a formally identical fashion regardless of the entities involved'.[108] One of the aims of the investigation was to try to find some method of identifying similar concepts so that in an information retrieval system the same fundamental concept could always be given the same piece of notation; thus the 'motion' part of heat transfer and the flow water in a pipe would be identified in the same way. Clearly any method which attempts to do this will be of help, and general systems theory is indeed the most general approach to the problem. The theory appears to have been applied first to obtain a reasonable order among the 'attributes' which included activities and properties as opposed to 'entities' to which the attributes might apply. Properties were considered to be more inherent than activities; an entity will continue to display the same properties whether it is involved in some activity or not. Properties thus precede activities in the overall sequence. Those properties which may be considered to be the result of subjective judgment are taken to be more general than those which relate to the physical nature of the entity, on the grounds that the former may be applied to the latter as well as to the entity itself; for example, we may refer to a beautiful flower or to a beautiful blue flower, but we may also refer to a beautiful blue. There are also some terms which may qualify any attribute; these general relative terms come first in the sequence of properties, which thus becomes:

General relative terms
    Degrees of amount
    Degrees of order of rank
    Degrees of kind or substance
Positions
    Time
    Space
    Person as user or possessor
Physical measure
    Mass
    Linear measure
Shapes
Appearances
    Light
    Colour

Sounds
Tactile sensations
Flavours
Odours
States
    Mechanical
    Energy
Structures

Activities were ranked in a somewhat similar fashion, the key feature here being the idea of 'degree of interaction'. This gives a general to special order beginning with static systems and progressing to the degree of interaction which leads to the emergence of new systems:

General activity concepts
General static and kinetic conditions
Equilibrium
General kinetic conditions
Contacts and disturbances
Motions and transfers
Assembly and disassembly.

RELATIONSHIPS BETWEEN CONCEPTS

While the theory of integrative levels and its development had given means of compiling a linear sequence of concepts, there still remained the problem of how to specify compounds of concepts and still retain the desired sequence. If we regard an entity as a system, systems theory gives a useful definition quoted by Austin: [109]

'A system is a set of objects (subsystems) together with relationships between them and their attributes. Since a system never occurs without an environment, a characterisation on this basis is incomplete without reference to the total system, *ie* the system plus its environment. All systems have thus to be identified by means of constraints which delineate their true positions and that of their subsystems vis-a-vis the environment.'

If we wish to establish a unique place for each possible combination of concepts, then we must define uniquely the relationships between them, and we must therefore introduce some kind of relational operators or role indicators. (These two, though slightly different in their practical application, are in fact merely different ways of expressing the same relationship. $A \ r \ B = R_1 A . R_2 B$, where r is a relational operator, R a role indicator.) The definition of a system indicates that we have to take into account the relationships between the system and the environment, the system and its attributes, and the system and its subsystems, and this gave the first three role indicators:

(1) Attributes of system
(2) Environment of system
(3) Subsystems

The indicators may themselves be compounded to show, for example, an attribute of a subsystem (31).

When we come to study the relationships between systems, a further important point emerges. In such an interaction, one of the systems may be regarded as active, the other as passive; a survey of a number of examples showed that we normally regard the passive as the primary system. This is in line with the well-established classification principle that when we have one subject influencing another, the primary topic is the one influenced.[110] For example, the influence of the classics on French art of the seventeenth century is classified with other works on French art, not with other works on the classics. A product arises from an operation within a system or between systems and thus should follow them in sequence (principle of consecutiveness). These considerations led to a revision of the simple idea of subsystems and analysis of the operator (3) into three separate operators:

(3) Active subsystem
(4) Passive subsystem
(5) Interactive between parts/Phenomena (*ie* Products)

If we consider ' self-activities ' within this framework it becomes clear that in fact all activity of a system takes place relative to the environment of the system, even when the latter is not explicitly named. It was therefore thought correct to introduce an operator for Activities, placing this *after* the operator for the environment. Further analysis suggested however that two different situations could be identified: one in which activities led to a change in the system, and another in which they did not. At this stage, the set of operators read as follows:

(1) Properties of system
(2) Second system/Environment related to (3)
(3) Activities and interactions not involving material change
(4) Active subsystem
(5) Passive subsystem
(6) Interactions within system

(7) Second system/Environment related to (8)

(8) Interactions involving a change of system.

One further stage was reached during this period of the research. The problem of distinguishing an attribute of an entity from that entity defined by the attribute had caused some difficulty. How can one distinguish, say, the domestication of animals from domestic animals, *ie* animals defined by having been domesticated? Another operator (9) was introduced with meaning 'attribute defining a sub-class', and an important decision was taken, that all activities should be expressed in the passive voice, *ie* as effects related to the passive system. Thus, if we were to have notation R for animals, and v597 for domestication, we would be able to distinguish the two topics quite easily, while still retaining the ability to search the file for each concept, using the same symbol wherever it occurs:

R(3)v597   Domestication of animals

R(9)v597   Domestic animals.

There was also some thoughts on the introduction of an operator (o) to introduce the idea of 'observation', *eg* such concepts as analysis and measurement, but at this point the grant ran out and further work was temporarily suspended. A great deal of the ground work had been covered, and the theories had been tested out on examples chosen from BNB. Austin rejoined the staff of BNB, and was able to continue the work, with a slightly different emphasis.

THE NEEDS OF BNB

The MARC project[14] had emphasized the need for any retrieval tools used with it to be consistent and logical. It also required collaborating organizations to standardize their practices as far as possible to that information could be exchanged on an international basis. With the latter point in mind, BNB decided to adopt the eighteenth edition of DC when it appeared, despite the fact that in some ways it would compare un-favourably with their own modification of DC14. However, this introduced a problem in indexing the class numbers. BNB had been using chain procedure to index their version of DC, but it seemed likely that use of DC18 would lead to problems of consistency which would require considerable programming effort if the index was to be useful or indeed usable. It was therefore decided to make use of the CRG work to produce, not a classification scheme, but a means of generating formal statements in words of the subjects to be classified. This decision shifted the emphasis of the work away from the problem of order, towards the problems of relationships between concepts. (Since an alphabetical system was involved, the order in which concepts will be filed is pre-determined.) These formal statements were to be manipulated by computer to give all the index entries needed, that is, each significant term was to be brought to the front of an index entry. However, instead of dropping terms as is the practice with chain index entries, the new method would preserve them in such a way as to demonstrate the full subject statement at all points.

PRECIS

The new system was given the name PRECIS, from PREserved Context Indexing System. It began with the CRG operators, modified again to give the following set:

(0) Observation—the observer, his techniques and equipment
(1) Property, structure, material
(2) Subsystem
(3) Interaction within system
(4) Second system related to (5)
(5) Effect produced upon system—'normal' events and system maintenance
(6) Second system related to (7)
(7) Effect produced upon system—metastatic change or 'detrimental' effects.

Operator (9) was not thought necessary because an alphabetical system was to be used. In a classified system, the same piece of notation would be used for an attribute considered as such and for that same attribute used to define an entity, as was shown by the example 'domestic animals' above; the only distinction would lie in the operator introducing the piece of notation. However, for a system using words, there would very often be a difference in the word form, as there is in the example quoted, which would make the operator redundant. (9) was therefore replaced by a comma to give the 'focus, difference' relationship.

The attempt to distinguish 'normal' effects from 'detrimental' effects soon ran into difficulties. In view of the problems which had already been encountered in investigating the 'pathology' approach, it is perhaps a little surprising that the attempt was made at all. Further consideration led to the conclusion that 'environment' is the role which is most general, and this was therefore moved to bring the environment to the beginning of the string of terms in every case. Subsystems, structure, material, properties and percepts were seen to apply more than once in a string denoting a complex subject, and they were removed from the main sequence of operators to an alphabetically designated subset. Bibliographical and physical form were also introduced into this subset, as was the idea of 'target' audience, Ranganathan's bias phase. Field membership, quasi-generic relationship, was another new feature, shown by /. This led to a revised set of operators, as follows: [111a]

 (a) Form, physical or bibliographical
 (b) Target
 / Field membership
 , Difference
 (p) Subsystem, structure, material
 (q) Property, percept
 (o) Study region, sample population
 (1) Viewpoint, perspective
 (2) Active system
 (3) Effect, action
 (4) Key system [*ie* passive or possessing system]
 (5) Discipline
 (6) Environment
 (v) Coordinate concept
 (w) Coordinate subject (comparison phase)
 (x) Coordinate subject in same document

The numerical operators were used retroactively. All statements had to contain either a system (4) or an activity (3)—since all concepts are defined as being either an entity or an attribute. (p) and (q) could be used wherever appropriate.

As experience has been gained in the use of PRECIS for the index to BNB, for indexing films for the *British National Film Catalogue*, and in various experimental collections of abstracts and research reports in special fields, further modifications have been made to the system of operators, though the underlying methodology has proved to be sound and has not been modified significantly. The set of operators currently in use is as follows[111b]:

  o Environment
  1 Key system
MAIN 2 Action

LINE	3	Agent
OPERATORS	4	Viewpoint
	5	Sample population; study region
	6	Target; form
INTERPOSED	p	Property or part
OPERATORS	q	Quasi-generic member
	r	Aggregate

The main line operators, denoted by numbers, are set down in ascending order, rather than retroactively (though the result, of course, is very similar). As before, all statements must contain a key system or an activity, but these are now coded 1 and 2. The interposed operators cannot begin a string, but may thereafter be inserted at any point, as before. It is possible to repeat certain main line operators to give the equivalent of Ranganathan's 'rounds'; in some examples, strings of twenty or more terms have been constructed without difficulty to give specific indexing of, say, scientific reports.

PRECIS has now been used for the subject index to BNB since the beginning of 1971, and has proved extremely successful. The system of operators is backed up for indexing purposes by a thesaurus showing hierarchical relationships between concepts, *ie* those relationships which exist between concepts as a result of their definitions and are thus not in any way dependent upon their occurrence in a set of documents. Its significance for UDC lies in the fact that the successful use of this set of operators gives an indication of one way in which the construction of new schedules for UDC might be undertaken, which will be further explored in the next chapter.

THESAUROFACET

Another key development from the CRG work has been the compilation of *Thesaurofacet*,[112] the fourth edition of the English Electric Company's classification of engineering and allied subjects. This has several interesting features which might influence future work on UDC.

The first of these is that *Thesaurofacet* represents a return to the idea of a thesaurus as it is exemplified by perhaps the best-known: that of Roget.[113] This consists of a *classified* list of terms with an alphabetical index; the term 'thesaurus' has been used in information retrieval to describe an alphabetical listing of terms, frequently of a kind which would better be called 'list of subject headings', were it not that this designation has undesirable connotations for some people.[114] *Thesaurofacet* consists of a classification scheme combined with an alphabetical index, the two being complementary. This would not in itself be worthy of note, since it is standard practice; the index to *Thesaurofacet* is however a ' thesaurus ' in itself, and does much more than simply indicate the notation for particular terms.

It has always been a criticism of classification schemes that they could only show one hierarchical relationship for any given concept; we can only show more than one such relationship by enumerating the concept more than once. These multiple occurrences should be collocated by the alphabetical index, but this does not always prove completely satisfactory. This is particularly so in the case of a scheme such as UDC, which does make some attempt to cut down unnecessary enumeration by use of the colon to link notational elements from different parts of the schedules. For example, it we wish to find information on ' paint thinners ', we can begin the search by looking in the index to UDC, where we find the following entries:

Thinners, paints 667.629.2

Paint(s) 667.63

    readymixed 667.63

Paint removers 667.69

We can get to the correct notation by looking under either Paint or Thinners; the latter leads, in correct chain procedure fashion, to the specific piece of notation, while the former leads, again correctly, to a broader heading, where we have to search through the schedules to find the point we want, which we can do without difficulty. It will be seen from the brief excerpt from the index that we might be discouraged by finding a direct entry (*not* according to chain procedure) for Paint removers; this might lead us to expect a similar entry for Paint thinners, and to give up the search when we do not find it. If we turn to the class number given, we find:

  667.629   Auxiliary ingredients; solvents, thinners, etc

      .2   Solvents and thinners: spirits, etc

The use of the word ' solvent ' here might lead us to consult the index again under that term, when we shall find:

Solvents 542.6, 66.062

    for paints 667.629.2

Only by following up this line of thought shall we find the rather surprising information that ' solvents ' is one of the common subdivisions to be used throughout 66 Chemical technology (though evidently not in 667.6). There does not appear to be any route whatever by which we could be led to one of the most commonly used paint thinners, turpentine, for which the class number is 668.48, unless we already knew that it was used for this purpose.

If we carry out the same kind of search in the index to *Thesaurofacet* we find it far more helpful. All kinds of relationships are shown, not merely species-genus or similar containing head relationships (*eg* thinners, paints: this shows the context within which the notation 667.629.2 denotes *thinners*). If we turn to ' thinners ' we find:

Thinners *use* Solvents

Turning to ' solvents ' we find:

Solvents	HXG
UF	Thinners
RT	Dispersants
	Dissolving
	Plasticizers
	Solutes
	Solutions
	Solvent extraction
NT(A)	Paint thinners
	Turpentine

The index thus shows us not only that if we are using an alphabetical system the preferred term is Solvents, but also the class number and a number of relationships which are not displayed by the classified arrangement. The classified arrangement does however display what are considered to be the primary relationships in the usual way. *Thesaurofacet* can be used for pre- or post-coordinate indexing systems, since it can serve as a source of terms or of class numbers; in either case, it displays relationships more fully than any other method. The ' hierarchical listings ' given in other thesauri, *eg* the EJC *Thesaurus*,[42] show hierarchies, but do not list the terms within them systematically.

Another interesting point in *Thesaurofacet* is the return to a discipline-oriented scheme. The first three editions of the English Electric classification scheme adopted the approach being pursued by the CRG: an attempt to list concepts without restricting them to a particular discipline, by applying facet analysis to the whole of the subject area to be covered. Despite the attraction that this might be expected to have for users who are working in a multi-disciplinary environment, it did not succeed and the fourth edition has gone back to a basis in the traditional disciplines. It should be remembered that the CRG work has always been oriented towards mechanized information retrieval, and has never been put forward as a practical scheme for shelving books. The classification part of *Thesaurofacet* could very well be used for this purpose. Since UDC has in the past served both purposes, it may be necessary to come to a decision on its future role before any significant progress can be made on its revision.

A further point, which could be of particular significance in relation to UDC, is that *Thesaurofacet* is no longer entirely synthetic in its notation. Synthesis inevitably leads to lengthy notation,[115] which is itself undesirable. Furthermore, there will be certain subjects which contain more than one concept, and therefore have to be represented by more than one notational element, and which nevertheless occur very frequently. This means that commonly occurring subjects have long notation, or at least longer notation than is necessary, which has to be made up on demand each time. (The latter point should not be exaggerated; a classifier would of course keep a record of each composite piece of notation used, and it would only be necessary to consult this record each time.) In order to avoid this, *Thesaurofacet* gives some of these subjects brief, non-expressive, notation; it does however also give the method whereby similar subjects, not foreseen by the compilers, can be accommodated through the usual synthetic devices. In a recent description of the scheme, Jean Aitchison points out that non-expressive notation is more convenient for shelving and similar purposes because it is shorter, but for machine searching it is much less satisfactory than expressive notation, since the machine has to be programmed to recognize each hierarchy individually—a very considerable effort, which BNB decided not to undertake, as has already been stated.

The notation of *Thesaurofacet* has also been simplified. In the earlier editions, upper case letters were used to denote facets, lower case letters to denote foci within facets, and also certain common facets; arabic numerals were also used. *Thesaurofacet* uses only upper case letters and numerals 2 to 9. The reason for this is quite simply the ' consumer resistance ' to the mixture of upper and lower case letters; despite their familiarity, there is no doubt that these symbols are not popular as notation.[116] Much of the appeal of DC lies in its very simple notation; if UDC is to survive, care must be taken that its notation does not become even more complex than it is already, and any simplification would certainly lead to increased acceptability among users.

4

SUMMARY

This chapter has set out to highlight some of the work of the Classification Research Group which could be of value in the future development of UDC. An attempt has been made to select certain aspects of the CRG work, and the examination is not by any means exhaustive; comprehensive accounts can be found elsewhere, and are listed in the bibliography. The points emphasized in this discussion are those which the present author believes represent significant ideas on which a procedure for the revision of UDC might be based. These include: levels of integration; time and causal dependence; role indicators; combination of schedules and thesaurus/index; a trend towards simplification of notation; a decision on the future purpose of UDC, which will dictate the whole structure and will affect the choice of notation.

CHAPTER 7

PROPOSALS FOR THE FUTURE DEVELOPMENT
OF UDC

The previous chapters have raised a number of questions, some of them relating to the detailed expansion of UDC, others to its use, and others casting doubts on its future validity as an information retrieval tool. In this chapter, proposals will be set out as potential answers to these questions.

OBJECTIVES

Before we can determine a future pattern for UDC, it is necessary to establish the objectives that have to be fulfilled. Is such a scheme necessary for the future? What exactly will be its functions? Are other information retrieval methods likely to take its place, particularly if computers become a standard tool in libraries?

NEED FOR GENERAL CLASSIFICATION SCHEMES

Despite the doubts that have frequently been expressed about the future utility of large general classification schemes, there seems to be little doubt that they are likely to continue in existence at least for the lifetime of libraries in their present form. While we permit readers direct access to our collections, we have to arrange these collections in some helpful fashion, and classification will continue to be the answer: it seems reasonable to try to ensure that classification schemes remain valid, and that standard class numbers for documents should be available from a central source.[47] The MARC record will obviously become more and more significant as time goes by, and will serve as a source of class numbers in this way, reinforcing the role played currently by

BNB and Library of Congress cards. Certainly those closely concerned with the large general classification schemes currently in use do not show any signs of pessimism when writing about the future of their scheme.[117] The UDC, as a scheme used by a great many libraries, must enjoy its portion of this security of tenure; it is not known exactly how many libraries do use UDC, as estimates vary, but the number must be many thousands, especially as UDC is obligatory in most East European scientific and technical libraries at least.[118]

At present, UDC numbers appear in a few places, but there are no firm plans to include them in MARC records, although there is a tag vacant for this purpose in the format. In this country the only difficulty is one of cost; in the USA more serious difficulties might be found, arising from the small numbers of libraries interested in, and librarians capable of, applying UDC. Nevertheless, one can foresee the inclusion of UDC class marks in the MARC record in the not too distant future if a sound case can be made out for this.

This is however not the main future that is seen for UDC as a general classification scheme. The point has been made that there is a great need for the international exchange of scientific information; if words are used as subject descriptors, problems of language arise which can be avoided by the use of an internationally recognizable symbolism. The original need which led to the development of UDC exists today in even more acute form, and UDC is clearly the scheme best suited to serve this purpose of those existing today. It has editions in some twenty languages all told, and the machinery for maintaining them, albeit imperfect, does exist; furthermore, UDC is the only scheme developed in sufficient detail for scientific information retrieval; its only competitor, Colon Classification, is still in too underdeveloped a state to be a serious rival.[119]

The SRC concept might be said to conflict with this view, but in fact such a clash may not necessarily occur. The SRC is seen as a broad classification only, whereas UDC is essentially a detailed scheme. SRC is seen as a 'switching code' to indicate general subject coverage; it is assumed that within each general subject so delimited there will be detailed analysis by some other indexing language or languages. Means by which SRC and UDC can be completely reconciled have been described, and a practical method of achieving this is described later.

General classification schemes will also continue to be needed to reinforce specialized indexing languages, as has been described in chapter I. Here again, because of its emphasis on detail UDC has an advantage over other existing schemes for this purpose. It also has the advantage of using arabic numerals for the main part of its notation; whatever the advantages of alphabetical symbols, numerals appear to be more acceptable, and certainly have a wider international currency.[116]

SHELF CLASSIFICATION OR INFORMATION RETRIEVAL?

If it is accepted that these needs exist, and that UDC can meet them, it remains to be stated that there can be conflict between the constraints of various needs. For shelf classification notation should be reasonably brief and easily comprehensible; it is for this reason very largely that BNB has decided to adopt the eighteenth edition of DC and abandon its own expansions of earlier editions.[120] For information retrieval through surrogates the Cranfield Projects and many others have shown that one of the most important features of an indexing language is its specificity; with a scheme such as UDC specificity can be achieved, but at a cost of lengthy notation. Can these two opposing factors be reconciled in one scheme? There are obvious difficulties, but a possible solution is put forward involving the SRC/UDC combination, discussed in detail later. Even in its present form UDC offers both full and abridged editions; it is feasible to use the abridgement for shelf marks, reserving the detailed schedules for information retrieval purposes, without any very great difficulties.

STABILITY OR CHANGE?

Another conflict arises out of the constraints resulting from different purposes: that between the librarian's need for stability in his arrangements and the need to accommodate changes in knowledge and its structure. In many ways this is a more serious conflict than the notational problems discussed above. There is no doubt that readers welcome a degree of stability as well as librarians, as witness the outcry whenever a library is rearranged! On the other hand, the position has now been reached in UDC where many of the schedules are so out of date as to be unworkable; a good example is Chemistry, where the present schedules are based on an approach which is no longer accepted by chemists.[121] It has been pointed out that the pace of change is accelerating,[122] and this leads to the conclusion that librarians will perforce have to accept a degree of flux in their shelf and catalogue arrangement.

There is already an acceptance of the fact that abstracting and indexing services do not cumulate indefinitely; if it were similarly accepted that library catalogues can no longer represent in one sequence all the holdings of the library, much of this particular conflict would be eliminated.

However, this idea does not lend itself so well to shelf arrangement; it is not practical to have a number of sequences by date open to direct access, especially if some of them will, with the passing of time and withdrawal of out of date materials, become relatively small. The use of a broad classification could help here by making the need for change less acute; it is usually in their details that classification schemes are first susceptible to obsolescence. Here again, UDC in its present abridged/ full versions, or the proposed SRC/UDC combination, could provide a valid solution. (It would also be possible to make a rule that a sequence on the shelves would cover a stated period, say ten years; once a new period began, the previous stocks would be transferred to the stacks. This might cause difficulties for a year or two, and is not recommended as a workable solution as it stands! It may however be claimed that it contains a grain of truth; we should be less concerned than we are with providing an overall sequence including everything, and more concerned with ensuring that the arrangement we do provide is a helpful one.)

LINKS WITH COLLECTIONS OF LITERATURE

UDC is the only one of the three major classifications (major, that is, in the sense of being most widely successful) that is not tied to a collection of literature; both DC and LC are developed through the daily work of classifying the books received by the Library of Congress. UDC gains its contact with literary warrant through the revision procedure, which puts the responsibility for the drafting of new schedules on the shoulders of those using the scheme in their libraries. This is sound, in that these are the people most in touch with the problems, but it also poses many problems. Many of the people using UDC in their libraries do not possess the rather specialized skills required for classification construction, and their efforts therefore tend to be enumerative and self-centred. By self-centred here is meant that each schedule is developed in isolation, with little reference to the rest of the scheme, and in consequence we have many of the duplications and anomalies that lead to external criticism. If UDC were linked to a large collection of literature, with a classification team responsible for the allocation of class marks and the development of the schedules, this would surely lead to an improvement in the revision process.

Such an opportunity may lie in the current development of the bibliographical services of the British Library.[123] It seems likely that this institution will take over the functions of BNB as part of its responsibility, and will have some funds for research and development. The use of PRECIS for subject analysis has been shown to be a help in classifying by DC,[120] and there is no reason to suppose that UDC would prove more difficult; indeed, if the intellectual revision procedure is revised as well as the mechanical, UDC may well lend itself rather better than DC to this approach. It is therefore proposed that the British Library should accept as one of its responsibilities the maintenance of a team to maintain and utilize UDC in this way. This would have the added advantage that a UDC class mark would appear in any MARC records generated in this country. If similar action were taken in other countries, with FID/CCC serving as the international clearinghouse, UDC would have a revision procedure second to none, and a much firmer base in literary warrant than is the case today, when, as Wellisch and others have pointed out, many revisions are used only by those who produce them while other areas desperately in need of renovation remain untouched for lack of effort.

MECHANIZATION

There is no doubt that computers will soon be used for a great many library operations presently performed manually. Two ways in which it has been suggested that UDC might be affected are through use in mechanized information retrieval systems and through computer production of the schedules. It is important that any developments in UDC should bear these points in mind. It has been shown in chapter 5 that both are feasible with current UDC, but there is no doubt that both could be performed more efficiently if future plans for UDC were to be made with mechanization specifically in mind. This would affect for example, the choice of facet indicators and similar notational devices; it suggests that the notation should be expressive as far as is possible, that is, it should reflect hierarchical divisions in the schedules. It implies the use of rigorous analysis in the development of new schedules and the avoidance of anomalies. Here again we see the need for a skilled team, thoroughly in touch with current thinking in both mechanization and classification theory, to be responsible for the development of the scheme, and the British Library suggests itself as the place where such combinations of skills are most likely to be available in this country.

FORMAT

If we accept the arguments put forward that UDC should continue to exist in the future as a viable general classification scheme, we have next to consider the format it should take. Should it continue to be made available in three different editions? How should new schedules be compiled to fit into the future structure? Should it remain as a traditional, discipline-oriented scheme, or should it become a new type of scheme along the CRG lines? In this section, some suggestions are put forward as answers to these and similar questions.

FULL, MEDIUM OR ABRIDGED?

In the previous chapters, arguments have been presented in favour of the medium edition (Wellisch) and to show that there is no means of determining on theoretical grounds how to abridge the full edition to give either the medium or abridged, which therefore suggests that the correct edition to produce is the full, from which users can abbreviate to suit their own purposes. Lloyd has also argued in favour of the abridged editions, which have, as he points out, been 'a godsend to countless thousands of UDC users'.[124] The proposed SRC is to be a broad classification, with perhaps some 5,000 divisions.

With thought it may be possible to reconcile these opposing views, to arrive at a solution acceptable quite widely, though like all compromises it may not exactly match any of the specifications. The distinction between full and medium editions is probably more apparent than real. It is important to remember that the full UDC schedules are in most cases still enumerative; this involves a great deal of repetition of concepts at various heads, which becomes unnecessary if the scheme is to be analytico-synthetic, as will be described in the following pages. The contrast between the two types of schedule in terms of length can be quite startling; the present author has pointed out[125] that a brief schedule containing four facets, each of which contains four concepts, can give a possible maximum of 624 headings, which would of course all have to be listed in an enumerative scheme if it were to be equally specific. If UDC were to become completely analytico-synthetic, the full schedules as they exist today would disappear, and their place would be taken by a very much shorter edition, to correspond with the present medium edition.

The SRC should become a list of basic classes in which only concepts falling into the primary facet should be listed. This proposal is based on the suggested use to which SRC is to be put, that of a broad switching language indicating the subject area (Dahlberg's subject fields) only, without detail. If we consider the 5,000 divisions provisionally put forward as adequate in this light, and remember that part of the scheme is to be a list of basic entities, if recent proposals by Lloyd are adopted,[126] it will be seen that they compare reasonably well with the present 12,000 divisions in the abridged edition, many of which again are unnecessary enumerations of composite subjects.

The future UDC should therefore consist of a broad classification fulfilling the function of the SRC and at the same time replacing the present abridgements, with a detailed analytico-synthetic scheme to replace the current full/medium editions and to expand the SRC. The SRC would correspond to the present main headings, *eg* those printed in bold type in the current BS1000A, but considerably revised, while much of the present detail in the full edition could be reduced by simply applying facet analysis.

One major argument that has been put forward against the introduction of SRC is that it conflicts absolutely with the need for stability of current users, a point discussed under the heading Objectives. To resolve this, it is proposed that the notation for the new SRC should always be followed by a semicolon before detailed subdivisions are added, and that a similar device be introduced into the present schedules. This would give a situation analogous to that described in chapter 4 relating to the use of N by UKAEA to denote Nuclear science and engineering. It was there suggested that N could form part of the SRC, with the rest of the schedule forming the full UDC expansion. If the semicolon were used as suggested here it would be entirely within the discretion of the user whether he adopted the SRC notation or continued to use the UDC notation as it is now. The semicolon is proposed for this purpose as it is one of the few symbols not already in use as an indicator by UDC. A similar suggestion has been put forward by Schmidt,[127] but his proposal depends for its effect on the fact that the SRC should use up to four digits without a point, rather than the three of UDC. However, this would not appear to be as satisfactory as the

4*

proposal made here, since it might on many occasions be necessary to add expansions to three-digit numbers which will also form part of the hierarchies of SRC. The more positive use of the semicolon seems preferable within the context proposed here. It should also be noted that this proposal could be put into effect *before* large-scale revision of the full edition has taken place, or it could be used to distinguish new detailed schedules from the old UDC base numbers before SRC comes into existence. In libraries wishing to adhere to existing UDC and ignore SRC and also future revisions of UDC, the semicolon would also be ignored.

It would obviously take both time and effort to introduce the kind of revision proposed here, but the scheme could continue with the minimum of disruption while revision was under way. The use of the semicolon delimiter would give the flexibility required without any risk of confusion.

It must be recognized that if large scale revision takes place, either of the basic class structures or of the detailed analysis, all users must eventually accept the changes or cease to use the current scheme altogether. Some may choose the latter path; a survey carried out in Britain some years ago showed that some libraries were still using editions of DC earlier than the fourteenth, even though the sixteenth, some thirty years more up to date, was available.[128] However, one cannot cater for ever for those who choose to opt out of change altogether. The proposal made here is intended to help those who wish to change to a new SRC as soon as it is available, but also those who decide not to make such radical changes at once.

ORIENTATION TOWARDS DISCIPLINES

It has been shown that a serious disagreement has arisen over the shape of any new classification scheme; should it reflect a primary arrangement by discipline, or should it follow CRG ideas and consider discipline only as a 'last resort'? The argument against basing a scheme on discipline is easy enough to state: disciplines are essentially rigid and reflect a point of view that is in the process of being superseded. It is true that many scientific advances fit uneasily into a discipline-oriented scheme; molecular biology is perhaps the best-known example, but many others can be found. The pattern of development within a discipline, where new subjects arose by 'fission', seems to have been replaced to a considerable extent by the new cross-disciplinary process of 'fusion'; whereas Dewey was able to cater for the former by his infinitely expansible decimal notation, he could not make any kind of provision for the latter. UDC has used the + sign to join class numbers from separate areas, and Schmidt and De Wijn[127] have proposed the use of the circumflex as the 'sign of fusion'. These methods do give a class mark, albeit a clumsy one, but they are evidently a makeshift. A discipline which is in existence before the scheme is compiled has a straightforward class mark; one that arises after the scheme is compiled is denoted by a different kind of class mark—yet both are essentially the same. There is of course also the point that a composite class number of the kind envisaged would not necessarily locate a new discipline in its correct place in the schedules: notation would dictate order.

The CRG has put forward powerful arguments to support its plans for a scheme free from the constraints of disciplines, and these constraints are very real; yet *Thesaurofacet*, compiled by a leading member of the CRG, reverts to the traditional division by discipline because it was felt that this gave a more helpful breakdown, and one with which the users were more at ease.[129] PRECIS includes Discipline as an operator in the set most recently published; in the revised set, it has been removed, but discipline is still normally shown by means of the thesaurus of semantic relationships. It appears that there is still a need for disciplines to be shown, and this is not unexpected if we recall that they reflect the way most subjects are taught throughout the educational structure. It is therefore proposed that UDC should remain basically a discipline oriented scheme as at present, but that provision should be made for the revision procedure to make specific arrangements for the inclusion of new disciplines as they arise. This would normally be at the SRC level; because of the way in which new disciplines are likely to arise, detailed analysis will need to wait until a degree of stability has been reached, but it may well be possible to 'borrow' details from existing schedules, particularly those of the parent disciplines.

THESAUROFACET FORM

One objection frequently raised to the use of classification schemes is that their linear structure cannot reflect the polyhierarchical relationships which occur between concepts; only one hierarchy can be displayed at the time.[130] The *Thesaurofacet* format enables the classification scheme to overcome this problem, as was shown in chapter 6. It is therefore recommended that future UDC schedules should be developed in this form: a classification scheme accompanied by a thesaurus, rather than by a simple alphabetical index. This could have a number of advantages in addition to the immediate gain in concept relationship display. In order to compile such a scheme, concept analysis has to be that much more precise; it is not sufficient to recognize one relationship only. This must lead to an improvement in the schedules themselves, since many of today's problems arise precisely because analysis in the past has been inadequate. The format would also help to obviate unnecessary duplication of detail between schedules, regarded by Schmidt as inevitable.[131] Such duplication often exists because it is the only way of showing multiple relationships, which could be done very easily by the thesaurus.

A question that would have to be resolved arises from this suggestion. At what point would the thesaurus section be constructed? If we consider the construction of a schedule for a single basic class, that is, a homogeneous field which can be analysed into facets, the problem of multiple relationships is much less likely to arise than if we are compiling a schedule for a broad subject area such as Engineering. This suggests that the compilation of the alphabetical section would have to be undertaken by a central body with complete control over the final schedules, even if construction of schedules for specific subjects remains as at present in the hands of individual users working through subject panels.

OVERALL ALPHABETICAL INDEX

The above proposals would also solve another problem 'at a stroke': the current lack of an alphabetical index to the whole scheme. As has been mentioned, there is no general index to the full schedules, and a few of the individual parts have been published without indexes, though happily this has now ceased as a matter of policy. If the compilation of a thesaurus-type index were regarded as an integral part of the exercise, this would only have any real meaning in relation to the scheme as a whole, as has been demonstrated in the previous paragraph. The task of integrating all the separate indexes has hitherto been regarded as impossible for lack of staff and finance; however, if the scheme becomes fully analytico-synthetic this will itself reduce the task considerably, since the number of individual concepts to be indexed will itself be strikingly reduced. The resulting publication would certainly be a great deal more manageable than the present full edition, both physically and intellectually.

SCHEDULE COMPILATION

Comments made so far have been devoted to the format in which schedules should be produced and the purpose for which they may in future be used. We have now to consider exactly how the revised schedules are to be compiled. Again, it is possible to argue that if the instructions for schedule revision had been adequate, so that the scheme was kept up to date more effectively, many criticisms would have been avoided; this is therefore a key area.

REVISION OF FID MANUAL

Section 2 of the FID Manual is quite inadequate as it stands, as has been shown in chapter 2, and must be revised. The exact form of the revision will depend, however, on the procedure that is adopted in future for the maintenance of the schedules. If the present decentralized methods are retained, rather more detail will be required than will be the case if revision passes to the control of a strong central body such as the British Library. Whichever way things develop, sound guidelines will be needed, and recent classification theory, including the ideas developed by the CRG and expounded in chapter 6, will be the main source of these. There will also be a distinction between the overall basic class development and detailed expansion within classes if the SRC idea is adopted, as has been suggested.

There is however no point in trying to make this section of the manual into a textbook of classification theory; such a venture might well be counterproductive, in that those consulting it might well decide to ignore it rather than struggle with a lengthy discussion. There should however be reference to such textbooks so that users can consult them if the need arises; at present, the manual has no references to other literature. Instructions should be as short as possible while retaining enough detail to make them usable. Perhaps the most useful way to start would be by suggesting that those not reasonably familiar with schedule construction should leave it to those who are!

No matter which way UDC develops, it is clear that there is a need for more centralized effort; it is no longer possible for such a complex scheme to be maintained by the very limited staff now employed. A much greater degree of control over schedule construction will be necessary, and to some extent this makes an improved manual redundant; however, it will always be easier to edit schedules if they are well constructed to begin with, the more so if all are constructed along the same lines. A suggested revision of the FID Manual was put forward two years ago, and a further revision of this is included here as Appendix D.

DEGREE OF DETAIL

One of the points of criticism of present expansions has been that they are too detailed; many of the subdivisions will be used only by those proposing them, and can hardly justify a place in a *general* classification scheme.[73] How detailed should new schedules be? Some indication of this must be given in the revised manual. One proposal put forward in the suggested revision referred to above was that terms should be based on the document collection being analysed and should not be more specific than this; reference tools such as dictionaries should also be scanned, as should existing classifications. This could lead to an unnecessarily high degree of detail, which Lloyd has suggested belongs more properly in a thesaurus or special classification. It has to be remembered that UDC is a *classification* scheme, that is, a means of arranging like things together; we should not lose sight of the wood of grouping in our search for the trees of superspecificity! It is therefore proposed that this instruction should be modified in the way that the EJC Thesaurus compilers modified the input to that listing. A large number of indexing languages in the relevant subject fields were collected and merged; from this total listing of some 150,000 terms, nearly 18,000 eventually were selected as descriptors. In a great many cases, a term was eliminated because it had only been found in one list; terms which were found in several lists were generally accepted.[132] We can therefore lay down a guideline that a term should not be included in a proposed schedule unless it is included in (say) three standard dictionaries covering the subject. There is a risk here that new terms may have to wait for general acceptance before being included; one is reminded of the fact that it took the Library of Congress more than a decade to admit that Cybernetics was a legitimate addition to its *Subject headings* list! The library has still not accepted the word Computers[133] after some twenty five years of constant use. There is however a simple but effective solution to this problem already available in UDC: the use of verbal extensions. The use of alphabetical subdivisions forms one of the common auxiliaries; in the English abridged edition it is specified to denote the names of individuals or firms, but there is no reason why it should not be used in the situation described above. This method has already been tried with success by Rigby, as mentioned in chapter 5, and it seems appropriate to make it a part of the formal revision mechanism.

ANALYSIS INTO FACETS

With a little practice, facet analysis becomes relatively easy, but to some at least of the users of the manual it will represent a completely new technique. Guidance will therefore have to be given on how the facets present in a subject should be identified, and which of them is to be regarded as the most important. It is in this section that the work of the CRG is most applicable. A preliminary analysis into entities and attributes will help to clear the air; one can then begin to identify key systems, actions, agents, parts, properties, etc. In view of the success of PRECIS in indexing the wide range of subjects covered by BNB, there seems to be no reason why the use of this kind of analysis should be restricted to science and technology, as have most of the guidelines drawn up in the past. Once the facts have been established, rules such as ' class at the passive system ' will help to indicate the primary facet, and indeed a complete citation order.

In subjects where it is found that some facets appear to recur, the use of matrix analysis as suggested by Caless for classifying (chapter 5) can be a useful aid. For example, one may have properties of things, where the things fit into the key system category, but at the same time also have properties of agents, where the agents perform some action on the key systems. The use of Caless's form of analysis rather than Ranganathan's Rounds and Levels is recommended because the former are considerably more precise; it is relatively straightforward to identify Things and Agents, but rather more difficult to recognize that both are Personality, one being first round, the other second or later.

COMMON FACETS

At this stage it will be important for common facets to be identified. One of the features of all the proposals put forward for the revision of

UDC has been an improvement in, and rationalization of, the common auxiliaries. We have already seen a significant step forward in recent years in the introduction of the common facets for Persons and Materials—one of the few major steps forward in this direction since the start of UDC, for the rest of the common auxiliaries were present at a very early stage of the scheme's development, as was shown in chapter 2. Proposals for the SRC have also included a list of General Object Entities[126] which would to a large extent replace the present UDC common auxiliaries:

Fundamental and formal entities
Energy and matter entities
Products, natural and artificial
Persons
Organizations
Nations, peoples, races
Languages, cultures, etc
Countries, regions, etc

It is of course essential that concepts falling into one of the existing common facets should not be duplicated unwittingly in a revised schedule, for it is in just this fashion that much of the overlap between divisions in the main schedules and those in the point of view schedules has arisen, as well as overlap between facets in different parts of the main schedules. Specific reference to this point must therefore appear in the manual.

ORDER WITHIN FACETS

There are a number of standard rules for arranging concepts within a facet; as these are included in most textbooks they will not be discussed here.[134] In chapter 6 it was suggested that two further ideas might be of value: levels of integration, and time and causal dependence. The idea of levels of integration, and the CRG elaboration of this to include levels of aggregation, is similar to the established rule of ' increasing complexity ' but is more useful because it is more precise, and indicates how one can identify increasing complexity. Time and causal dependence are also of value in indicating the order in which concepts within a facet should be arranged. These ideas are of course also likely to show their worth in developing the order of basic classes which will make up the SRC or revised UDC superstructure. Since the ideas themselves are somewhat complex, it will be necessary to include simple examples in the manual to demonstrate how they may be applied.

NOTATION

The present UDC notation is universally admitted to be clumsy as well as lengthy. This arises from a variety of causes: lack of synthesis, leading to the repetition of base numbers in colon combinations, *eg* 621.384.634.415 : 621.318.3 : 621.311.6; lack of modulation in drawing up the original schedules, necessitating use of the stroke to insert intermediate headings, *eg* 243.72/.73; mixture of symbols to indicate different facets, *eg* 546.33'13–145.061:621.039.84 = 03.82 = 20. (It should also be pointed out that in the last example just quoted, .0 in 621.039 is *not* a facet indicator, but merely a device to find a class mark for Nuclear engineering within 621 : yet one more confusion.)

Various solutions have been put forward, and several have been discussed in earlier chapters. The use of letters, adopted by Freeman and Atherton, worked very successfully but introduced symbols normally excluded, and is therefore not recommended. Schmidt and Dahlberg have both suggested revision of the notation for auxiliaries using fewer symbols, and this seems to be a more practical method. Certainly there is little scope left for *increasing* the number of symbols; there can be very few on the standard typewriter keyboard still left unused! (The use of the semicolon in the way suggested earlier would remove one more of those few remaining.) It is also important to bear in mind the need for notation to lend itself to computer manipulation in future systems; this suggests that the notation should be expressive as far as is possible. It is not possible to reconcile expressiveness indefinitely with the more important need for hospitality, *ie* the ability to allot notation to new subjects in their correct places in the overall order, but an analytico-synthetic scheme is less likely to suffer from this problem than one which tries to enumerate, simply because ' new ' subjects often consist in fact of new combinations of concepts already listed.

The proposal put forward here is that for a major revision, the number of indicators should be reduced to six or seven. The means by which this can be achieved are as follows, bearing in mind that some of the suggestions could be put into effect straight away. All common auxiliaries, *ie* those which are applicable at all points, should be introduced by a comma followed by one of the numbers from 0 to 9. The table of common auxiliaries would then appear as follows:

,1   Language
,2   Bibliographical forms etc
,3   Place

,4   Time
,5   Point of view (if these are retained)
,6   Materials
,7   Persons

This retains the filing order which exists at present. If the new set of General Object Entities is adopted, the notation would be similar:

,1   Fundamental and formal entities
,2   Energy and matter entities
,3   Products, natural and artificial
,4   Persons
,5   Organizations
,6   Nations, peoples, races
,7   Countries, regions, etc

The use of the comma indicates a common auxiliary, while the number following it dictates its filing position within these facets. Considering each facet in a little more detail, current notation could be used with a minimum of alteration, or in some cases none at all other than the change of indicator. Bibliographical forms would retain their present notation, *eg* (084.3) would become ,284.3. Place, Language, Point of view, Materials and Persons would require some minor changes to retain the point demarcating three-digit blocks, *eg* (425.42) would become ,342.542 and –053.8 would become ,738. For Time, the three-digit blocks are already ignored in giving dates, so the ,4 might well be followed by a point for visual convenience: "1972.09.13" would then become ,4.1972.09.13.

Facets within a subject should have their notation marked off in a similar way, but using the hyphen to replace both – and .o currently used. As has been shown, there does not appear to be any significant difference in the way these two symbols are used, and they can therefore be merged into one. A class number for a composite subject would therefore consist of the base and notation, taken from the appropriate facets introduced by –1, –6 or whichever is correct. To give the minimum of alteration from present usage, .o might well be replaced by –o; this could be done now without causing any confusion, and would eliminate one source of confusion existing at present, were it not for the recent introduction of the –03 and –05 common auxiliaries!

The suggestions put forward above would cause a minimum of clashing with existing notation. The use of the hyphen is simply a reinforcement of present practice, while the comma, which is not used at all at present, could be introduced unambiguously. The recommended changes could therefore be introduced gradually, as the appropriate sections of the scheme are revised.

The stroke and the plus sign would be retained with meaning similar to that currently valid. A complete revision of the basic outline would presumably remove the need for the stroke to show steps of division which have been overlooked, but it would still be needed to show new disciplines growing by fusion of existing disciplines which appear side by side in the schedules. Similarly, the plus sign would be used to show new disciplines arising from the fusion of non-contiguous disciplines. It should *not* be used to show subjects which happen to occur together in a particular document, as has been explained in chapter 4. Square brackets should be used for grouping as suggested in the chapter 4 discussion on bonding; if Wellisch's rule is accepted, square brackets will only be needed in exceptional cases; they should be used to enclose any + combination, to show that it is indeed a single entity which is referred to. Molecular biology might, for instance, be designated [57+539.19] with any subdivisions added only after the square brackets. This would be in line with the suggestion for designating ' science and technology of . . .' proposed in Appendix B.

The sixth indicator is the colon. This symbol is so much a part of UDC that its omission would surely render the scheme unrecognizable! The majority of relationships would be catered for by the comma and hyphen, linking facets to the appropriate base numbers; there will however always be examples of relationships which do not fall into this category, in particular the ' phase relationships ' first identified by Ranganathan. These are the relationships which arise between concepts which do not fall into the same basic class: influence, comparison, exposition, bias, to use the terminology adopted by BNB.[68] There will be a need for an indicator to cater for these, and the colon would serve this purpose.

A possible seventh is the recently-introduced double colon, intended to show subordination. If the schedules are correctly worked out to begin with, the need for this indicator will be greatly reduced, but it could be retained to serve its present purpose in certain circumstances. A concept may well be qualified to show *kind* by using descriptors which would not normally be associated with it permanently; this is Austin's Focus-Difference relationship. This can also occur as a new subject area develops, where this method of differentiation may well be used as an interim measure pending the development of a new schedule. The use of the double colon would distinguish these relationships from the phase relationships mentioned in the last paragraph, *eg*

621.318.3 : : 536.48	Cryogenic electromagnets [focus-difference]
621.318.3 : 536.48	Electromagnets for use in cryogenics [bias phase]
621.3.036.61 : : 621.791	Welded electrodes
621.3.036.61 : 621.791	Electrodes for welding

The proposals given here, and included in the revision of the manual given in Appendix D, are an attempt to reach a compromise acceptable to both those who want far-reaching and radical changes and those who, while expressing some slight discontent with the current state of UDC, wish to see the scheme continue largely as it is at present. They do not solve all the problems, but it is believed that they could give a procedure which would enable progress to be made.

SCHEDULE PUBLICATION

It has been clearly shown, not only in the present discussion but in many others also, that it is absolutely essential for the methods used for schedule publication to be improved. Present methods are slow, and have a built-in tendency towards obsolescence; when it is so difficult to make sure that the schedules one is using are the latest, there is a strong inducement to use those which are most conveniently to hand. Many studies of the ways in which readers use libraries have shown that they will take the item which is most easily obtained, even if another item appears to be more suitable, if the second item is likely to take some time to get.[135] This approach, if applied to UDC schedules, accounts for the fact that the English abridged edition has been reprinted at regular intervals, even though the latest amendment date is 1963, and many of the schedules have been completely superseded.

Within this area, many writers have put forward suggestions; the proposals here build on these earlier plans, but go somewhat further. The situation will also be changed if UDC becomes fully analytico-synthetic, since schedule production will then be rather less complicated and lengthy.

MECHANIZATION

Freeman and Atherton showed clearly that UDC schedules can be produced automatically by computer-controlled typesetting, using the length of the symbol to dictate the type face. At present this has some snags, as the notation in many places is far from expressive; if in the course of revision this point is borne in mind, it should be possible to arrive at a situation in a few years' time where the schedules can be produced by this method very nearly as well as by the most careful intellectual editing. (The editing will, in fact, have gone into the schedule construction stage.) All that will be necessary will be to maintain the schedules in machine readable form, *eg* magnetic tape. The major advance proposed here is that the output should be in the form of Computer Output Microfilm (COM) rather than hard copy. This was discussed in chapter 3, and it appears to the author to be the solution to this particular problem.

REVISION PROCEDURE

The difficulties experienced with the present methods of publication of revisions have led to a new proposal being put before the FID/CCC at its September, 1972 meeting.[136] P-Notes, which have a very limited circulation at present, are to cease to serve as anything more than drafts; *Extensions and corrections* will cease to exist when the present series reaches its final cumulation (covering 1971-1973) and will be replaced by an annual volume of *Supplements,* which will itself cumulate into five-yearly volumes. These five-yearly cumulations will be in two versions, intended for the users of the full editions or the medium and abridged editions respectively. It is difficult to see what advantages are to be gained by this change; the annual volumes will not cumulate progressively as do the present *Extensions and corrections,* and by the end of four years users are going to be faced with a worse situation than at present. On the proposed plan, by the end of 1978 it will be necessary to check the cumulative *Extensions and corrections* for series 1-5, series 6, 7 and 8, and then four volumes of annual supplements! Such a procedure is so impractical as to be almost incredible. Of course, one would hope that before 1978 the full and medium editions of the English version would be available, eliminating the need to go back to early series of amendments, but one is forced to the conclusion that the whole philosophy behind the proposal is at fault.

The introduction of COM would mean that at the end of each year a complete new edition could be published, incorporating all the amendments proposed during the previous year and completely obviating the need for annual supplements. Indeed, it is doubtful whether it would be necessary to publish halfyearly *Extensions and corrections* if users knew that everything would be available in a comprehensive form at the end of each year. Publication schedules could be speeded up; at present, the issue of *E & C* covering any given year is not published before September of the following year, and such a delay would be quite unnecessary if COM were to be used. Costs would need to be carefully controlled, but in view of the large numbers of copies of UDC schedules sold, it would seem that there is a market sufficiently large to make the project sound economically, without considering the vast improvement from the point of view of the user wanting up to date schedules.

Some users would also be able to utilize the magnetic tapes, which would become available as a by-product of the COM operation, for their own information retrieval systems, possibly using them to replace the conventional schedules altogether. It may seem somewhat futuristic to think of libraries making use of schedules in this form, but AUDACIOUS showed that it is already well within the bounds of practical possibility, and with current economic trends towards cheaper machines and more expensive people, many libraries are having to revise their ideas about introducing computer techniques.

A further point arises from the earlier proposal that there should be a radical rethinking of the role of the full, medium and abridged editions. If the attitude expressed here is accepted, that there is no theoretical or practical justification for anything other than a full edition, there is no point in having two different supplements. The revised, analytico-synthetic, UDC will in any case be more compact than the current full schedules, leaving even less scope for different editions; the only distinction will lie between the SRC/Superstructure, corresponding to some extent with the present abridgement but intended solely for use as a shelf classification or switching code, and the full schedules intended for use in information retrieval. Since it will be possible to show both on the COM version, distinguished by the semicolon delimiter suggested earlier, one edition will be all that is required.

MANAGEMENT

Many of the problems of UDC have arisen from inadequate management; Wellisch has made perhaps the most telling attack on this, as was shown in chapter 4, but the same theme is to be found in many of the other proposals for reorganization. If UDC is to move forward, it must be revitalized at the centre; the present staff of one full-time classifica-tionist is simply not enough, even with help from other organizations and individuals.

One suggestion that has been made relates to the constitution of the Central Classification Committee, or rather to its function. At present it has considerable executive responsibilities, but as Schmidt[131] has pointed out, the more frequently it meets, the more often its members have to miss meetings! The CCC is made up of delegates from many countries, giving their time voluntarily; it is difficult for many of them to spare the time, or obtain the money, for frequent attendance. Much of the work is necessarily done by the Executive Group FID/CCC/EG, consisting of a limited number of members who are normally able to attend all necessary meetings. Schmidt suggests that the Executive Group should undertake in future much of the work done at present by the CCC itself. It should meet five times a year, for a week at a time, in order to have adequate time to get through the business in hand. The Classification Secretariat would then be responsible for keeping the machinery rolling according to the instructions of the Executive Group. Since this consists of the editors of the major full editions, this sugges-tion would appear to be a reasonable one, but it still leaves much of the essential work to a part-time committee. Wellisch, however, suggests that there must be a full-time head editor, with a team of three or four experts, also full-time, to assist him.[73] We may compare this with the team of seven who spend their time revising the *Dewey Decimal Classi-fication*, though it should be remembered that UDC does have its net-work of international subject panels who can be consulted.

The proposal made earlier in this chapter that the British Library should take over responsibility for the development of the English edition would give just such a full-time team of classification experts, who would have access to subject experts also, either within the British Library or through its nation- and world-wide links. The English edition could then become the basis for all versions of UDC, editions in other languages being prepared under the supervision of the FID/CCC chief editor. Policy would remain in the hands of the FID/CCC: a situ-ation analogous to that of DC, where the work of revision is carried out in the Decimal Classification Division of the Library of Congress, but overall policy is decided by the Forest Press Inc, acting on the advice of the Decimal Classification Editorial Policy Committee.[137] It could be argued that such an arrangement would remove the control of UDC from the hands of the organization originally set up for that purpose, the FID. However, with the CCC retaining control of editorial policy, and FID directly responsible for editions in languages other than English, a sound working arrangement could surely be reached. The team at present working within British Standards Institution, which again is a fairly small one, could be transferred to the British Library, or BSI could retain its responsibility for the actual publication—though it is in the British Library that the necessary expertise with COM is more likely to be available.

This proposal may seem both chauvinistic and unfair to the two organizations concerned, FID and BSI. On the first ground, it is not unfair to point out that, if there is a *lingua franca* in existence today, it is English, which is used for a substantial proportion of all scientific and technical literature, and is understood by many people who have a different mother tongue. On the second ground, it is perhaps not unfair to point out that the present state of UDC is not a particularly good advertisement for the two bodies concerned; both have been hampered by lack of funds, but if they have found it difficult or impossible to raise funds, then it seems we must turn to some other body more likely to succeed in this respect.

FINANCE

Reference has been made at various points to costs, and the problems of obtaining funds. In chapter 4 some possible sources of funds were considered, without any very hopeful answer arising, but there do seem to be two possible sources of finance for UDC. The first of these is the proposal that it should come under the umbrella of the British Library, at least as far as the English edition is concerned. The funding required for a UDC Division, corresponding to the Decimal Classification Division, would be relatively small in relation to the overall costs of the library, and there would be certain advantages to be gained, such as the inclusion of UDC numbers in the MARC record. The second source of funds would arise from the sale of the completed edition; Wellisch indeed believes that this could finance the whole operation if it were pursued vigorously, particularly if the US market could be opened up. The proposals made here for the regular publication in magnetic tape and COM form of an up to date edition would almost certainly lead to a steady income, though whether this would be sufficient to finance everything would depend on pricing policy. If, say, 5,000 sets could be sold annually at a price of £10 this would mean an income of £50,000, a substantial part of which would be profit: certainly enough to maintain a greatly enhanced operation. The seventeenth edition of DC has sold nearly 40,000 copies,[138] which makes it a best-seller by any standard; if UDC could approach this figure, there would be no need to worry about finance.

CONCLUSION

This chapter has tried to set out a series of proposals which, if adopted, could lead to a resurgence in the UDC. The solutions put forward have so far as possible been chosen to fit into the present pattern with a minimum of dislocation, though obviously changes in management such as those suggested in the previous section would involve a major change in the overall organization. The present situation, where revision of UDC is in effect conducted on the basis of a world-wide gentlemanly old-boy network, is becoming intolerable, and users must accept a much greater degree of centralization if the scheme is to survive beyond the next few years. What is essential is to arrive at a *reasonable* solution to the many problems; if this can be found, it will be accepted, even though it may be imperfect. If change is delayed still further in the hope that a perfect solution can be found, that solution may arrive too late to be of any use.

CHAPTER 8

SUMMARY AND CONCLUSIONS:
HAS THE UDC A FUTURE?

There have been many ready to announce the death, sudden or long drawn out, of general classification schemes. The *Dewey decimal classification* from which UDC gains its overall structure received[139] an obituary in 1955, but could well claim, as did Mark Twain in a similar situation, that 'the reports of my death are greatly exaggerated'. UDC itself received what might have been considered a death blow in 1961 with the publication of the Kyle/Vickery reports to Unesco, yet it has refused to succumb; more importantly, its users have refused to allow it to succumb. The meeting organized by Aslib in London on July 6, 1972,[140] referred to in chapter 4, showed that there is still considerable interest among librarians using the scheme in Britain; similar interest is reported by Schmidt for German users. The question that has to be answered is: can the UDC serve a useful purpose in the future, or not? If so, what steps have to be taken to ensure this?

If the answer is no, then nothing more remains to be said; there is no point in devoting time, energy and scarce resources to the support of a scheme which has no future. Better to let it subside gradually into obsolescence, to remain as a monument to the 'géniale invention de MM Dewey, Otlet et LaFontaine', a curiosity of interest only to the historian. The present author does not believe the answer to be no, and the theme of this study is that UDC does indeed have a future if the necessary steps are taken to ensure three things; revision of the schedules wherever appropriate, using modern classification theory; improvement of the management structure; adequate finance.

Improvement in the schedules is certainly needed. The overall structure (superstructure) is outdated, and many of the detailed schedules are equally in need of revision. However, it has been shown in several recent projects that UDC compares surprisingly well in its detail with the EJC *Thesaurus* (*TEST*); this work is reported in Appendix A, and demonstrates that some of the criticisms that have been made in the past are unfounded. Proposals have been made by a number of authors for the way in which UDC might be revised; these have ranged from fairly minor changes to the construction in effect of a completely new classification. We have tried in chapter 7 to put forward some suggestions that could lead to a thorough revision over a period of a few years, yet would not inconvenience present users so greatly as to deter them from using the revisions. A detailed proposal for a revision method is included as Appendix D, which in some respects goes back to the original ideas of Otlet and LaFontaine, notably in the use of the hyphen for all special auxiliaries.

Improvement in the schedules is of little use if their availability remains as poor as it has been in the past. In effect nobody has ever used the full English edition of UDC, because it has never existed, and will not until such time as all of the schedules have been published in their current state. New methods are available and must be adopted; here again, proposals have been made in the past, and further suggestions are made in chapter 7. There is of course no guarantee that they will be successful; all that one can say with certainty is that the present methods are not, and must be improved.

The state of the schedules, and the unsatisfactory publication programme, are themselves reflections of organizational weaknesses. Thirty years ago, perhaps, one man might be able to maintain the scheme by his own, almost unaided, efforts, though one may doubt even this; Schmidt[62] refers to the fact that Donker Duyvis occasionally mentioned that ' one should really start with the UDC again from the beginning ', but without being able to do very much about it. In today's environment teamwork has largely replaced the individual, and this must happen with UDC also. To some extent it does already happen; the revision procedure, with its subject committees and international subject committees and the Central Classification Committee, is designed to ensure that new schedules arise as the result of a consensus among those who eventually have to use them. The problem with this procedure is that it is organizationally too weak; time passes while committees deliberate and communicate, time that cannot be spared in many cases. In chapter 7 the proposal is made that the English edition of UDC should be one of the responsibilities of the British Library. This suggestion, if adopted, would have the very great advantage of linking

UDC to a large and active collection of literature, just as DC and LC are linked. If the author's calculations are reasonably correct, the operation could be made self-supporting; if Roberts is right in his statement[141] ' If one thing is certain, it is that the BLS will administer strictly limited funds ' then obviously this could be a significant factor!

Funds will have to be found for the revision and publication programme envisaged. No one has yet succeeded in finding a completely satisfactory answer to this problem; indeed, if an answer had been found much of what has been written here would be superfluous. The UNISIST meetings were ready to point the need for improvements, but apparently overlooked the need to will the means to this end. Yet the sums involved are relatively modest, even if they are not as modest as FID estimates imply. Interest in UDC in the United States, though relatively slight, does exist, as some of the work reported in chapter 5, and the issue of a recent bibliography,[142] have shown. A more active approach to its popularization in that country might well lead to a quite satisfactory increase in income from the sale of the English editions.

Perhaps the major factor to be taken into account at the present time is the SRC project. It is clear that this has had tremendous influence on FID thinking, and that the idea is with us to stay. Its effect on UDC could be good if it leads to the kind of revision that has been shown to be necessary; the fears expressed by many in this country relate to their doubts as to whether FID work on SRC is compatible with their commitment to UDC. This point has been discussed in chapters 4 and 7, and a proposal put forward that might serve to further both interests without building up hostility among present users.

In many ways, UDC now stands at a watershed in its existence. Is it to flow towards the Dead Sea of obsolescence and desuetude, or is it to flow towards that ocean of which Sir Isaac Newton wrote:

' I do not know what I may appear to the world, but to myself I seem to have been only a boy playing on the seashore . . . whilst the great ocean of truth lay all undiscovered before me '.

APPENDIX A

A comparison with the COSATI categories and EJC Thesaurus of engineering and scientific terms (TEST).

One of the major criticisms made of UDC is that it is not adequate to handle today's scientific and technical literature. In recent months there have been several investigations of this, which tend to show that UDC is in most cases perfectly adequate, but that some sections do need revision to bring them up to date. It is also important to remember that thesauri often contain very specific terms which one would not expect to find in a classification scheme; in chapter 7 it was shown that such terms can easily be inserted into UDC as verbal extensions, provided that there is a reasonable heading to extend.

Vickery's investigation[61] had apparently shown that UDC only contained about half the terms found in TEST in the areas compared. Unfortunately, the circulation of this report was restricted, and for some time its contents were only known through an article by Arntz.[143] With wider distribution, the conclusions have come under severe criticism, and other workers have obtained quite different results. Ohman[144] has pointed out that many of the concepts for which Aslib were unable to find UDC equivalents can in fact be classified quite easily; in some cases, an exact equivalent exists which must have been overlooked by the Aslib team, who were working with the schedules then available in 1969. Ohman himself found a much higher degree of agreement; in three areas investigated, Bosons, Crystals and Thermodynamic characteristics, Ohman was able to find UDC numbers without difficulty for 65 out of 70 terms where the Aslib team had only been able to find 38. However, in Medicine the situation was rather less satisfactory; only about seventy five percent of the terms taken from MeSH[145] could be accurately classified, a reflection of the fact that the UDC schedules for Medicine are badly in need of revision.

In the USA, Steuart[146] investigated the use of UDC as a source of terms in nuclear science and technology. As has been mentioned, this is one of the areas covered by a special subject edition, and is in many ways one of the most satisfactory areas in UDC. Using this edition and no other schedules at all, Steuart was able to find well over ninety percent agreement; this is in itself highly significant, but Ohman[147] has additionally pointed out that if a similar comparison is made of TEST and the Euratom Thesaurus[148] we find a much greater level of disagreement!

Wellisch[149] has carried out a pilot project on the use of UDC as a switching language to translate TEST into other languages, in collaboration with Ohman and I de Vries. The terms to be compared were taken from the Subject category index in TEST. This is a listing of all the preferred terms (*ie* excluding synonyms) in subject groups, which correspond except in a few minor details with the Subject categories formulated by COSATI[42]; the listing within each group is however not systematic but alphabetical, so that the groups form a very broad classification. 173 descriptors were selected from TEST as a carefully planned sample; of these, a UDC class number could not be found for only one: Queueing theory. This would fall into Mathematics, which is currently undergoing largescale revision. A further very interesting point to arise out of this study was that some eighty five percent of the descriptors could be coded quite satisfactorily using only the abridged and medium edition—the full schedules were only needed for the remaining fifteen percent. (This is the basis for Wellisch's assertion that the medium edition is the one that should become the main method of publication in the future.) The work of Wellisch and Ohman also showed that about one third of the descriptors in TEST are precoordinated to some extent; this confirms the present author's view that most of the lists graced by the title Thesaurus could equally well be called lists of subject headings, were it not that this term now has pejorative connotations.[114] Such terms can of course be catered for quite simply by the various synthetic devices in UDC.

A similar examination has been made for the purposes of this study, taking a schedule which shows some of the weaknesses of UDC: Computers. This corresponds to COSATI category 0902. The UDC schedule is a comparatively recent one, having been compiled in the late 1950's and eventually published as a P-Note in 1965. However, Computer technology is an area in which progress is startlingly rapid, and several concepts which have come into prominence in the 1960's are, as might be expected, missing from the schedule. An additional problem that arises is that the schedule is placed in 681.3; this identifies it hierarchically as falling within the division 681 Precision mechanisms of 68 Specialized trades, crafts and industries for finished articles and goods, which itself is part of 6 Technology. The schedule is therefore weak on Programming and Programming languages, which, it may be argued, do not belong in this area; this argument would be more acceptable if provision for them were made elsewhere but there is no sign of this.

The COSATI category contains some 178 terms, 16 of which are names of specific languages. This puts them into the category of ' identifiers ' rather than descriptors, and as such they have been excluded; however, given a satisfactory UDC number for Programming languages, specific languages can be inserted by using the normal alphabetical device.

The full edition schedule for Computers was used; this gives all the detail, but does not have an index, and it is possible that some class numbers may have been overlooked through this lack. Subjects falling outside 681.3 were classified by using the abridged edition of 1961; again, more up to date schedules might have proved more helpful in some instances. However, despite these difficulties, it proved to be possible to find a reasonable UDC equivalent for 106 of the 162 terms listed. The remaining 56 fall into two groups: those for which a UDC number can be found for a more general concept, ie the UDC number given is not specific; and those 7 for which no UDC equivalent could be found, or for which the UDC number given is suspect. The remaining 49 are those shown with an asterisk against the UDC number given; of these, 30 relate to programming and programming languages, and 5 to time-sharing and related concepts which have only arisen in the past ten years or so, since the schedule was originally compiled. It should also be pointed out that the UDC schedule does include a number of concepts which do not appear in the COSATI category, though some of these do appear in other categories, eg Function generators, and in all fairness it has to be admitted that some of the terms in the UDC schedule show its origin in the 1950's rather clearly!

These studies show that in general UDC compares satisfactorily with TEST, which is a much more recent compilation. They reinforce the premise maintained throughout this study, that there are no fundamental reasons why UDC should not serve as adequate indexing language for the future.

Terms from COSATI category 0902 Computers and suggested UDC numbers. * indicates a UDC number not as specific as the TEST term.

Table 1

Accumulators	681.325.54
Airborne computers	681.323 : 629.7
Analog computers	681.33
Analog to digital converters	681.34.053
	681.34'33'32.053
Aperture cards	681.327.45*
Arithmetic and logic units	681.325.5/.6
Assembler routines	681. 3.061*
Assembly languages	681.3.065*
Associative storage	681.327.6.071?
Asynchronous computers	?
Autocodes	681.3.065*
Auxiliary equipment (computers)	681.327
Binary processors	681.325.53.042
Bombing computers	681.3 : 623.557.027
Buffer storage	681.327.2*
Calculators	681.325.5
Card punches (data processing)	681.327.45'11
Card readers (data processing)	681.327.45'12
Card reproducers	681.327.45'13
Card sorts	681.327.45 : 681.325.67
Card to tape converters	681.327.45'12 : 681.327.44'11
Central processing units	681.325/.326
Character generators	681.327.11*
Character processors	681.325.3?
Character recognition devices	681.327.12*
Collators	681.327.45 : 681.325.67
Compilers	681.32.053*
Computer components	681.3–2
Computer driven punches	681.327.44'11
Computerized simulation	681.3 : 371.69
Computer logic	681.3.056
Computing gun sights	681.3 : 623.55
Consoles	681.326.73 (operating console)
	681.327.12* (visual display units)

General purpose registers	681.325.54*
Guidance computers	681.3 : 62 ...
Hollerith code	681.3.048(Hollerith)
Hybrid computer	681.34
Hybrid simulation	681.34 : 371.69
Index registers	681.326.33
Information systems	007
	02
Input output devices (computers)	681.327.13
Input output routines	681.327.13.06
Interpreter routines	681.3.06*
Interpreters	681.327.45'13
Keyboards	681.327.11*
Key punches	681.327.45'11
List processing languages	681.3.06*
Loader routines	681.3.06*
Logical elements	681.325.6
Logic circuits	681.325.6 : 621.372
Logic design	681.3.056
Machine coding	681.3.065.4.023
Machine oriented languages	681.3.065.4*
Macroprogramming	681.3.06
Magnetic cards	681.327.65
Magnetic disks	681.327.63
Magnetic drums	681.327.63
Magnetic heads	681.327.6'13
Magnetic storage	681.327.6 or 681.327.63/.66
Magnetic tapes	681.327.64
Mechanical computers	681. 31 : : 621
Merging routines	681.325.67.06
Microprogramming	681.3.06*
Monitor routines	681.326.7.06
Multiplexers	621.394.42
Multiprocessing	?
Multiprogramming	681.3.06*
Object programs	681.3.06.023
Operating systems (computers)	681.326.3.06
Optical character recognition devices	681.327.5'12
Parallax computer	681.3 : 623.55
Parallel processors	681.325*

Pattern recognition devices	681.327.5'13
Printers (data processing)	681.327.54'11
Printouts	681.327.54
Procedure oriented languages	681.3.06*
Programming languages	681.3.06*
Programming manuals	681.3.06(02)
Punched card collators	681.327.45:681.325.67
Punched card equipment	681.327.45
Punched card interpreters	681.327.45'13
Punched card readers	681.327.45'12
Punched card reproducers	681.327.45'13
Punched cards	681.327.45'22
Punched card sorters	681.327.45:681.325.67
Punched tape readers	681.327.44'12
Punched tapes	681.327.44'22
Punches	681.327.4'11
Radar range computers	681.3:621.396.969.1
Random access computer storage	681.327.6.025
Reader-punches	681.327.4'13
Readers	681.327.4'12
Reading machines	681.327.12
Read only storage	681.327.21
Recursive routines	681.3.06*
Registers (computers)	681.326.33
Report generators	?
Semiconductor computer storage	681.327.67*
Serial access computer storage	681.327.6.025*
Serial processors	681.325.3.025*
Shift registers	681.326.3*
Shipboard computers	681.3:629.12
Simulational languages	681.3.06:371.69*
Simulator routines	681.3.06:371.69*
Sorting routines	681.3.056
Source programs	681.3.06*
Special purpose computers	681.31
Subroutine libraries	681.3.06*
Subroutines	681.3.06*
Summary punches	681.327.4'11
Symbolic codes	681.3.04
Symbolic programming	681.3.06*

Synchronous computers	?
Tabulating equipment	681.327.44'11 : 681.327.5'22
Tape punches	681.327.44'11
Tape to card converters	681.327.44'12 : 681.327.45'11
Tape to tape converters	581.327.44'12 : 681.327.44'11
Thick film storage	681. 327.66★
Thin film storage	681. 327.66★
Time sharing	681.3.06★
Translator routines	681.3.06.023★
Twistors	681.327.66★
Utility routines	681.3.06★
Variable word length processors	681.325.3.065★
Verifiers	681.327.17
Word organized storage	681.327.2.053★

APPENDIX B

CLASSIFICATION OF SCIENCE AND TECHNOLOGY

There are various ways of arranging the topics which fall within the broad heading of Science and Technology. The UDC follows Dewey's lead in gathering together all of Science (with the exception of medical science) in one group, and all of Technology in another. At the other extreme is Brown's practice in the Subject Classification of collocating each technology with its basic science; this idea has often been ignored, largely because Brown's execution of it left much to be desired, but is seen in Colon Classification and in Bliss's Bibliographic Classification. Ranganathan follows Physics by Engineering, Chemistry by Chemical Technology, Geology by Mining, Zoology by Animal Husbandry, etc. Bliss collocates Chemistry and Chemical Technology, and some branches of Physics with their technologies—but then leaves the rest to go into his Useful Arts class towards the far end of the overall sequence. Colon also has a Useful Arts class which is something of a 'dustbin' collection.

It seems clear that there is no general consensus among the schemes. Literary warrant works both ways: one finds textbooks in which the various branches of Physics are brought together, but one also finds such works as the 'Sourcebook in Atomic Energy' which deals with both Nuclear Science and Nuclear Technology.

It is equally clear that there is no general consensus among the individuals concerned. In the main, a mechanical engineer will have more in common with an electrical engineer than with a physicist interested in Mechanics; an electrical engineer more in common with a chemical engineer than with a physicist interested in Electricity and Magnetism. This is however by no means always the case: a vacuum physicist and a vacuum engineer will have much in common, as will a solid state physicist and an electronics engineer working with transistors or integrated circuits.

In UDC the use of the $+$ may provide a way out of the dilemma within the existing framework, by enabling us to specify both the science and the technology of a particular topic, *eg,*

539.1 + 621.039	Nuclear science and technology
533.5 + 621.52	Vacuum science and technology

This is the use of the $+$ to indicate a genuine aggregate class, but it is open to some theoretical objections. These can best be demonstrated by considering the overall order resulting from its use.

The arrangement in *figure 1,* which is that arising from the straightforward use of the plus $+$, obviously gives an overall order in:

5/6	Science and technology
5	Science
5 . . .	. . .
53	Physics
. . .	. . .
533.5 + 621.52	Vacuum science and technology
533.5	Vacuum physics
. . .	. . .
539.1 + 621.039	Nuclear science and technology
539.1	Nuclear physics
. . .	. . .
6	Technology
. . .	. . .
62	Engineering
. . .	. . .
621.039	Nuclear engineering
. . .	
621.52	Vacuum engineering

Figure 1

where Science comes between the general heading Science and Technology and the special-general headings Vacuum science and technology and Nuclear science and technology. On the other hand, the existing UDC notation does not lend itself to the arrangement given in *figure 2,* which does give the desired progression from general to special. To achieve a mnemonic effect, it would be necessary to have a parallel arrangement under the general heading Science and Technology and under the special headings Science and Technology; without this, it would be difficult to provide in advance for every possible literary warrant at the wider heading without a great deal of enumeration. This however implies that there is such a parallelism between Science and its related Technologies. I am not convinced that this is the case; even Colon Classification shows little parallelism within its parallel main classes, and other schemes show even less.

5/6	Science and technology
?	Nuclear science and technology
?	Vacuum science and technology
...	...
5	Science
...	...
53	Physics
...	...
533·5	Vacuum physics
...	...
539.1	Nuclear physics
...	...
6	Technology
...	...
62	Engineering
...	....
621.039	Nuclear engineering
...	...
621.52	Vacuum engineering

Figure 2

It may be that an approach using the Classification Research Group (CRG) analysis of entities and attributes, combined with integrative levels, would give a more satisfactory comparison, but I am inclined to doubt this.

I am in fact not at all sure that any solution which is both theoretically and practically satisfying exists, but it may be possible to use some device to give a satisfactory result with UDC. The use of [...] suggests itself as a possibility: the question marks in *figure 2* might be replaced by notation of this kind, *eg*,

5/6[535.5+621.52]
5/6[539.1+621.039]

The objections I see remaining to this are those which apply to the overall order within UDC; the divisions at 5/6 would parallel those at 53/54 (or possibly a wider set of the subdivisions of 5) and would therefore be open to the same criticisms. Since we have in mind the improvement (admittedly long-term) of this situation, perhaps we should go ahead and recommend the solution proposed here.

A third possibility might also be considered. Many works which require the use of the + in this way contain a minimum of the science —sufficient for the student to gain the foundations for a study of the technology. In such cases, it might well be desirable to file works on the science and technology of the subject immediately before works on the technology, *eg*,

621.039 + 539.1	Nuclear science and technology
621.039	Nuclear technology
...	
621.52 + 533.5	Vacuum science and technology
621.52	Vacuum technology

Any solution to this problem is likely to leave some users dissatisfied!

Reprinted from Caless, T W and others *Strategies for manipulating Universal Decimal Classification relationships for computer retrieval* (ref 27) p 21-23.

APPENDIX C

Infodata Systems Inc was founded in 1968, the President having previously been employed by Xerox Corporation, where he was the person
principally responsible for the development of DATRIX, the system used
for AUDACIOUS by Freeman and Atherton. The INQUIRE system would
appear to be rather similar to this; it has facilities for searching either
on keys (in the particular case examined here, these were keywords) or
sequentially on full text. As the UDC numbers formed part of the text, a
direct search for a UDC number had to be performed in the sequential
scan mode, which took rather more than ten minutes for the data base
of about 11,000 items. A search on keywords took only a few seconds,
and a compromise was reached for this demonstration; one keyword
was selected to reduce the number of items to be scanned, and searching
was then continued by means of the UDC numbers.

The date base used was *Abstracts and index of geological literature
excluding North America,* published by the American Geological Institute. The volume for 1967 was available in machine readable form;
apart from the keywords, the following information was included as
appropriate in non-keyed optional fields:

Field name	Field type	Maximum Length	Meaning
ACCESSNO	FIXED	0009	Index entry number
ABS-VOL	FIXED	0003	Index volume number
ABS-ISSU	FIXED	0003	Month of issue
PRISOURC	FIXED	0004	Source of entry
TITLE	VARIABLE	0300	Title
SUBTITLE	VARIABLE	0200	Subtitle

5*

SR-AUTH	VARIABLE	0060	First author
JR-AUTH	VARIABLE	0060	Second author
PRIJOURN	VARIABLE	0120	Journal
PRIVOL	VARIABLE	0120	Volume, issue, pages, illustrations, language (other than English)
PRIREF	VARIABLE	0060	Date (possible also continuation of PRIVOL)
UDC-NO	VARIABLE	0075	UDC number
CAT-NO	FIXED	0002	Category number (the index is arranged in 19 broad categories)

To conduct a search, the enquirer has to state the search terms. Keywords are stated after the word FIND, using Boolean operators AND, NOT and OR if necessary. A particular year of publication can be searched by using the form FIND Y-1967; similarly, a language may be specified by using FIND L-FRENCH. UDC numbers to be searched are defined within quotes: UDC NUMBER CONTAINS ' 55:001.4 '. The items found can be printed out in two ways, using the TAB or LIST. Using TAB, the enquirer states the fields he wants; if no positions are given, the standard tabulator settings are columns 1, 12, 22, 32 etc but these can be overridden if necessary:

TAB ACCESSNO * ABS-ISSU * CAT-NO * UDC-NO *

gives the following layout:

ACCESSNO ABS-ISSU CAT-NO UDC-NO
E67-11163 12   19 $551.243:550.838(571.5)=03.82=20$

This can be varied by stating the tab positions:

TAB ACCESSNO 1 ABS-VOL 12 ABS-ISSU 21 CAT-NO 31 UDC-NO 39

gives the following layout:

ACCESSNO ABS-VOL ABS-ISSU CAT-NO UDC-NO
E68-17112 32   12   02 $553.81:549.211:552.323.6$

If no instruction is given, or if LIST is used, the whole entry is set out in formal fashion:

DATA FILE ITEM   6421
ACCESSNO E67-06647
ABS-VOL   31
ABS-ISSU 8
PRISOURC S
TITLE   REMARKS ON SOME ORDOVICIAN CONODONT FAUNAS FROM
          WALES

SUB-TITLE
SR-AUTH   BERGSTROM, STIG.M.
JR-AUTH
PRIJOURN   ACTA UNIV. LUNDENSIS, SEC. 2
PRIVOL   NO. 3, 67 P., ILLUS.
PRIREF   1964
UDC-NO   56.016.3 : 551.733.1(429)
CAT-NO   14

Before starting a search, the enquirer may ask for COUNT instead of giving layout instructions. The computer will then perform the search and print out the number of items found; this can be useful, since it enables the enquirer to reformulate a search if the first attempt gives unduly high recall. If COUNT is not specified, the computer will nevertheless print out the number of items retrieved at the end of the search printout.

Example:

FIND USSR AND L-ENGLISH, COUNT
[Response]   195   ITEMS RETRIEVED

The program has a full quota of error messages. Examples:

110 ERROR   ' –20 ' IS ILLEGAL—SHOULD BE ' AND ', ' OR ', ' TO '
080 ERROR   NO PREVIOUS TABULAR DEFINITION EXISTS
075 ERROR   FIELD ' ACESSNO ' DOES NOT EXIST
' ORDOVICIAN ' NOT IN INDEX   (*ie* term not used as keyword)
NO ITEMS SATISFY THIS REQUEST

It is worth noting that the last message is somewhat negative in that it does not give any clue as to what would be a correct keyword; however, part of the system would be an alphabetical printout of keywords used to help in this selection.

A typical search showing the power of UDC for generic searching. USSR is used as the keyword to ' prime ' the system, as explained above.

FIND USSR AND UDC-NO CONTAINS '551.24' and UDC-NO CONTAINS — '(57' AND UDC-NO CONTAINS '=20', TAB ACCESSNO * ABS-ISSU * — CAT-NO * UDC-NO *

Response:

ACCESSNO	ABS-ISSU	CAT-NO	UDC-NO
E67–11162	12	19	551.243 : 550.838(571.5)=03.82=20
E67–11159	12	19	551.243(571.54)=03.82=20
E67–10005	11	19	551.243.1 : 551.763.1(571.64)=03.82=20

E67–09993	11	19	$551.243.3(571.53)=03.82=20$
E67–09846	11	19	$551.24:550.361.2(571.5)=03.82=20$
E67–09633	11	19	$551.243.31:551.3.051:551.782(575.3)=03.82=20$
E67–08594	9	19	$551.243/.3(571.61)=03.82=20$
E67–07471	8	19	$551.24(57-18)=03.82=20$
E67–07475	8	02	$553.981/.982:551.24(575.16)=03.82=20$
E67–07459	8	16	$552.53:551.24:551.732.2(571.5)=03.82=20$
E67–06966	8	19	$553.94:551.24:551.251(571.16)=03.82=20$
E67–07053	8	19	$551.243.1/.3(571.5)=03.82=20$
E67–07049	8	19	$551.24(57-15)=03.82=20$
E67–07012	8	19	$551.24:551.763/.78(571.66)=03.82=20$
E67–07064	8	02	$553.3/.9.061:551.243(574.4)=03.82=20$
E67–06953	8	19	$551.243.1(571.63)=03.82=20$
E67–06253	7	19	$551.24:551.71/.72:551.73:552.4/.5(574)$ $=03.82=20$
E67–06143	7	19	$551.243.1:552.4(574.4)=03.82=20$
E67–06396	7	19	$551.243.31(571.6)=03.82=20$
E67–06001	6	19	$551.243.3(571.1)=03.82=20$
E67–05045	6	19	$551.24:551.71/.72(571.5)=03.82=20$
E67–03210	4	19	$551.243.1(57)=03.82=20$
E67–01085	2	19	$551.243.1(574.42)=03.82=20$
E67–01072	2	19	$551.245:553.068:551.71/.72(571.5-13)$ $=03.82=20$
E67–01069	2	19	$551.24:553.042:551.73(575.21-13+470.5-13)$ $=03.82=20$
E67–01099	2	07	$551.331.5:551.24(575.21-17)=03.82=20$
E67–01088	2	19	$551.243.1:551.735(574.5)=03.82=20$
E67–00729	2	19	$551.243:551.734.5(574.3)=03.82=20$
E67–00714	1	02	$553.3/.4:551.244(571.54)=03.82=20$
E67–00743	1	08	$550.83:551.24(571.5)=03.82=20$
E67–00745	1	19	$551.243.1(57-11)=03.82=20$

31 ITEMS RETRIEVED

Notes. $=03.82=20$ shows a translation from Russian into English. Valid items are found whether they occur in category 19 Structural geology or not, provided that the UDC number for structural geology 551.24 appears (or, of course, any of its subdivisions). Similarly, the search is restricted to Asiatic Russia by specifying (57, but it identifies any of the areas within Asiatic Russia represented by subdivisions of (57. The decimal point has significance; searching for 571.2 would not match 625.712.6 (though 712.6 might!).

APPENDIX D

Proposed revision of Section 2 of *UDC revision and publication procedure.* (FID Publication No 429)

2.   CLASSIFICATION AND NOTATION PRINCIPLES

2.1   *Nature and scope of the UDC*

2.11   The UDC is a systematic and hierarchic scheme for classifying documents. It covers the whole of knowledge and uses a notation consisting mainly of arabic numerals, used decimally.

2.12   Every concept and each of its aspects should have a place corresponding to its range of application. Subjects not yet provided for can be found a place in the schedules by following the rules set out in this section. Premature division of a subject should be avoided; concepts which do not appear in the schedules can be accommodated temporarily by using ' verbal extensions ' as described in paragraph 2.293(2) until experience shows that a permanent place is justified.

2.2   *Basic classes and facets in the UDC*
     In the UDC, concepts fall into one of two distinct categories—primary, called basic classes, and subsidiary, called facets.

2.21   Primary concepts (basic classes) are found in the primary listing which forms the superstructure of UDC. They are given a two-, three- or four-digit notation which reflects their position in relation to other basic classes within a framework of disciplines. New basic classes will arise relatively rarely, and before proposals for addition to the superstructure are put forward the existing schedules should be carefully checked to see that the subject is indeed not already represented.

2.22   Each basic class will include a number of subsidiary concepts which may be grouped into *facets*; for example, in Literature there is a

Language facet, a Literary form facet and a Period facet; in Engineering there is a Kind facet (Electrical, Mechanical), a Products facet, a Parts facet, etc; in Education there is an Educand facet, a Level facet (primary, secondary, tertiary), a Persons facet, etc. The concepts within a particular facet all bear the same relation to the containing basic class; they are all distinguished by applying the same principle of division or differentiating characteristic.

2.23   Facets found within a given basic class may be of two kinds:
(1) Common facets, applicable to all or most other basic classes. Examples are Persons, Materials, Time and Place.
(2) Facets which are specific to the basic class under consideration. Examples are Literary form in Literature, Coolant in Nuclear reactor technology, Offences in Criminology, Social processes in Sociology.

2.24   Common facets are listed at the beginning of the schedules. Concepts falling into one of these facets are denoted by notation beginning with a comma, eg Leicestershire in the place facet has the notation ,342.542.
Facets specific to a particular basic class are listed in the schedules at the appropriate place for that class. Concepts falling into one of these facets have notation beginning with a hyphen, eg -31 denotes Oxides in the Type of compound facet in Chemistry, Novels in the Literary form facet in Literature, and Degree of ceremonial in the Liturgy facet in Religion.

2.25   A subject to be classed may be simple or composite, and composite subjects may be of more than one kind.
(1) A simple subject reflects only one facet of a basic class, or of course the basic class itself. Literature, Novels and English literature are all simple subjects.
(2) A composite subject consists of more than one concept, which may reflect the presence of several facets of the same basic class, or facets from more than one basic class.

2.26   The notation for a simple subject will be found by looking it up in the schedules, where it will be found enumerated. The notation for the basic class is given, and the piece of notation for a single concept is added to this for a single-faceted subject. Eg
        Mechanical engineering 621
        Rotary slide valves 621-32 (from Parts facet)

2.27   The notation for a composite subject has to be built up or *synthesized*. The notation for the basic class is found, and to this is added the notation for the other concepts present.

(1) When the other concepts all fall into either the facets of the basic class, or the common facets, the notation is simply added on according to the sense of the subject being classified, *eg*

        Mechanical engineering 621

        Clutches -578

        Safety devices -78

giving   Clutches on safety devices 621-78-578

        Safety devices on clutches 621-578-78

        Education 37

        Leicestershire ,342.542

        Secondary -33

giving   Secondary education in Leicestershire 37-33,342.542

(2) When other concepts present fall into facets from other basic classes, notation is synthesized using the colon, *eg*

        Education, 37

        Government legislation 351

giving   Influence of government legislation on education 37 : 351

        Influence of government legislation on secondary education 37-33 : 351

        Influence of government legislation on secondary education in Leicestershire 37-33,342.542 : 351

This device is used to show influence, comparison, exposition, or bias. Exposition is the use of one subject to explain another, *eg* a psychiatric study of Hamlet; bias is an indication that the subject is presented for a particular audience, *eg* pathology for nurses.

2.28   It may occasionally be necessary to use a double colon; this device is used when a concept is defined by means of a concept which is found in another basic class, *eg*

        Mechanical engineering 621

        Pistons -242

        Metallurgy 669

        Steel 669-18

giving   Steel pistons 621-242 : : 669-18

2.29   From time to time documents are written in which the subject represents a fusion of more than one basic class. When the classes represented are contiguous in the schedules, their notation is joined by a stroke; if they are separated, the plus sign is used. In both cases the resulting piece of notation is enclosed in square brackets to show that it is to be considered as a unit, *eg*

Manufactures [67/68]

Molecular biology [57 + 539.2]

2.291 Square brackets may also be used to show algebraic grouping. In any composite piece of notation, any element specifies the elements written at its left side up to but not including a colon or double colon. If such an element is to specify the elements beyond the colon or double colon, then those elements to be included must be placed within square brackets, *eg*

Aluminium 669-71

Paints 667.6

Artists' materials 75-232

giving   Manufacture of aluminium paint for artists

75-232: : [667.6: : 669-71]

Aluminium for the manufacture of artists' paints

[75-232: : 667.6] : 669-71

2.292 For visual convenience, lengthy notational elements are broken up into three-digit units by means of the point, which has no other significance, *eg*

667.6

,342.542

2.293 Parentheses may be used to enclose terms which do not appear in the schedules. These fall into two groups: names of individuals, and new concepts.

(1) Names of individuals are not normally listed in the schedules; example, the Literature schedule does not include the names of individual authors. They can be inserted whenever appropriate by using parentheses, *eg*

820(Shakespeare)   or 820(SHAK) etc

629.113(Ford)

(2) New concepts may arise for which no existing heading is satisfactory. Pending the revision of a schedule to accommodate them permanently, they can be used as terms enclosed in parenthesis, *eg*

681.327.64(twistors)

2.3   *Need for schedule revision and expansion*

Knowledge does not remain static, and schedules which are sound when first compiled may become out of date. In some subject areas this happens relatively slowly, for example Literature; in others it may happen very much more quickly, for example Physics. An out of date schedule is of little help in classifying a collection of current literature, and the need arises for the schedules to be expanded or perhaps completely revised.

2.31   Draft proposals for revision may be submitted by any UDC user through the mechanism described in sections 3 and 4 of this manual, but a word of warning is appropriate. The construction of a satisfactory schedule for a basic class requires some knowledge of the theoretical principles involved; knowledge of the subject, though obviously required, is not in itself enough to give good results.

2.32   If a new schedule is to be constructed, the following guide lines should be followed in order to ensure that the proposed changes fit into the overall pattern of UDC.

2.321   The basic class should be carefully defined by reference to dictionaries, encyclopaedias etc. The overall structure of UDC must be adhered to; a basic class to be fitted into Pure Science must not include Engineering, for example.

2.322   Concepts falling into the basic class so defined should then be identified by a careful study of the literature. After a few concepts have been noted, it is possible to begin to identify also the facets into which they fall. A preliminary division which may be found helpful is that into Entities and Attributes; a concept is either a thing or an activity. Entities may be further analysed into Things, Parts, Materials etc, while Attributes may be divided into Properties, Processes and Activities. The facets appropriate to any given basic class will usually be identified quite rapidly if this process of analysis is carried out.

2.323   Some of the concepts found in any basic class will fall into the already existing common facets. These should not be duplicated, and it is therefore necessary to study the existing schedules carefully to avoid such overlap.

2.324   A decision has to be taken on how many terms to include. If too much detail is included the schedule will become unnecessarily complicated, and it has been found in practice that excessive detail is not used. As a simple rule, a term should not be included unless it can be found in three dictionaries or encyclopaedias covering the subject area.

2.325   Once the facets have been established and all the required terms have been identified, it becomes necessary to impose order on the collection of concepts. Two different approaches have to be made, one to the problem of order within each facet, the other to the order in which the facets are cited in a composite subject.

2.325.1 There are a number of principles which can help in establishing order within a particular facet. These include:

chronological
evolutionary
increasing complexity
spatial
size
alphabetical (for concepts having specific *names*)
traditional

Other ideas which may be helpful are that of causal or time dependence, which suggests that a concept denoting a cause is filed *before* any concepts denoting its effects, and levels of integration. This is the theory which states that the whole is often more than the sum of its parts, since it includes an element of *organization* in addition; a concept denoting a higher level of integration should be filed after one from a lower level. This would indicate that in Parts facet for, say, automobile engineering, *engines* should follow items such as pistons.

3.325.2 For single entry systems it is necessary to establish a citation order, *ie* the order in which the elements constituting a composite subject are to be stated. Without such an order, there is the possibility of cross-classification, that is, placing the same composite subject in more than one place. For multiple entry systems, citation order is also necessary so that the original statement of the subject is semantically sound.

Here again there are a number of principles which can be used for general guidance. In terms of the generalized facets mentioned above, a standard citation order would be:

Things, Parts, Constituents, Properties, Processes, Operations, Agents.

There may of course also be Constituents of Agents, Parts of Agents, etc so that the sequence may begin again. In a complex subject of this kind, the use of a matrix may be of help in the analysis and in establishing the correct citation order. Relationships between facets should be expressed in the passive voice, *eg*

Systems (affected by) Agent

rather than Agent (affecting) System.

2.326 When the order within the facets and the citation order have both been established, the schedule can be written down. This should be done using the 'principle of inversion'; that is to say, the least important facet should be written down first, followed by the next least important, until the final facet is reached. This will be the *primary facet*, *ie* the one which appears first in the citation order. Only concepts falling into this facet will be grouped in a classified arrangement; concepts falling into subsidiary facets will be scattered.

2.33 Notation can now be allocated to the completed schedule. The basic class itself will be fitted into the overall superstructure of UDC at the most appropriate place to show its relationships with other classes. Notation for the facets will be allocated according to the number of concepts in each; if there are fewer than eight, single digit notation will be adequate, if more, two digits (centesimal) notation should be used. It is rare for a facet to contain more than a hundred concepts of equal rank; subordinate concepts should be shown by subdividing the notation, *eg* Crops in Agriculture:

1	Grain
11	Wheat
113	Spring wheat
. . .	
2	Root
21	Tubers
211	Potatoes etc

In general the zero should be avoided; this is so that additional concepts can be inserted at a later stage if necessary by using 01 to 09 as subdivisions.

2.331 The facets themselves must now be labelled using a hyphen followed by one or two digits, depending on whether there are more than eight facets. For example, if there are six facets in Agriculture, of which Crops is the most important, the notation for Wheat would be -611; this would be added to the notation for the basic class to give, say, 63-611 as the complete notation.

2.34 An index must now be compiled, in which all the concepts in the schedule are listed in alphabetical order showing the notation for each. Any synonyms should also be included at this stage. The method known as chain procedure should be followed; the essential point of this method is that it is not necessary to index subdivisions of a term under that term, since they can be found very easily through the schedule. In the example quoted in 2.33, index entries would be:

Crops	**63-6**
Grain crops	63-61
Potatoes: root crops	63-621.1
Root crops	63-62
Spring wheat: crops	63-611.3
Tubers: root crops	63-621
Wheat crops	63-611

Entries for Grain crops: wheat, or Tubers: potatoes, are omitted as redundant.

2.35 At all times the existing schedules must be kept in mind, both to aid the revision and to avoid unnecessary duplication and overlap.

2.36 The completed schedule should now be tried out on a reasonably large collection of literature. If it proves successful, it can be submitted as a draft to the appropriate committee.

The above instructions are compiled with the recommendations for notation made in chapter 7 of the text in mind. They could be modified very easily to fit into the present notational pattern. They are based to some extent on the proposal forming part of Caless, T W and others *Strategies for manipulating Universal Decimal Classification relationships for computer retrieval* (ref 27) modified to fit into the pattern of FID 429.

BIBLIOGRAPHY AND NOTES

CHAPTER 1

1 Dewey, M *A classification and subject index for cataloguing and arranging the books and pamphlets of a library. Amherst College, 1876.*

2 *Chemical abstracts* now includes over a quarter of a million items —periodical articles, patents, technical reports, etc—each year. B C Vickery has estimated ('Statistics of scientific and technical articles' *Journal of documentation 24* 1968 192-196) that there may be more than a million periodical articles in science and technology each year. In another subject area, *Research in education* lists some 12,000 items annually.

3 Coates, E J *Subject catalogues* (Library Association, 1960).

4 Coates, E J Private communication.

5 See, for example, CRG Bulletin no 7 *Journal of documentation 18* 1962 65-68; also Denison, B *Selected materials in classification* (Special Libraries Association, 1968). The latter is the latest publication of a list of special classification schemes maintained for some years by the Special Libraries Association and now forming part of the Bibliographic Systems Center at Case Western Reserve University.

6 Classification Research Group *Classification for library science* Preliminary draft edition (Aslib, 1966). The scheme has now been thoroughly revised in the light of experience gained at the College of Librarianship Wales, the Polytechnic of North London School of Librarianship and the Library Association. The first formal edition will, it is hoped, be published by the Library Association shortly.

7 MEDLARS, The MEDical Literature Analysis and Retrieval system, uses a list of subject headings, MeSH, published as part II of the January issue of *Index medicus* each year; this has an associated volume showing 'tree structures', *ie* classificatory hierarchies.

8 Austin, D 'Prospects for a new general classification' *Journal of librarianship* *1* 1969 149-169. Further references are given later when the work of the CRG is discussed in detail.

9 Brown, J D *Subject classification* Third edition revised by J D Stewart (Grafton, 1939).

10 Ranganathan, S R *Prolegomena to library classification* (Asia Publishing House, third edition 1967). This is Ranganathan's major theoretical work; the practical exemplification of his ideas on synthesis are seen in *Colon classification,* of which the first edition was published in 1933 and the seventh is expected shortly.

11 Bliss, H E *Bibliographic classification* (H W Wilson, 1940-1953). Bliss devoted more of his attention to the order of main classes than to detailed working out in the classes, but he did give a number of systematic auxiliary schedules which could be used for synthesis at various points. However, Bliss did not appreciate all the problems of notational synthesis, nor did he regard an all-synthetic classification as a practical proposition.

12 US Library of Congress *Classification* Class P Language and literature, published in parts 1909-1948; some of these have been republished with supplements, but the basic scheme remains in its first edition.

13 Foskett, A C *The subject approach to information* (Bingley, second edition 1971 *passim*).

14 US Library of Congress *The MARC II format: a communications format for bibliographic data* (1968).

Jeffreys, A E and Wilson, T D *The UK MARC project* (Oriel Press, 1970).

BNB/MARC Documentation Service *publications* include one on UK MARC.

15 Austin, D 'An information retrieval language for MARC' *Aslib proceedings 22* 1970 481-491.

Austin, D and Butcher, P *PRECIS: a rotated subject index system* (BNB, 1969). (BNB/MARC Documentation Service publication no 3.)

16 Freeman, R R 'The management of a classification scheme: modern approaches exemplified by the UDC Project of the American Institute of Physics' *Journal of documentation 23* 1967 304-320. This summarizes work carried out by Freeman and Atherton, published in detail as a series of reports by the American Institute of Physics (ref 81 below). The work is discussed in more detail in chapter 5.

17 Much of the historical material in this chapter is taken from the *Bulletin de l'Institut International de Bibliographie 1-3* 1895-1898. Volumes 1 and 3 contain lengthy papers by Otlet and LaFontaine single and jointly): volume 2 begins with an introduction to the *Classification Décimale* followed by an abridgement containing about 1,500 headings taken from the 40,000 already to be found in the main schedules, and an index. It is perhaps salutary to see that many of the ideas relating to notational synthesis and citation order which we tend to think of as relatively new were in fact already quite well developed by 1895.

18 Hopwood, H V ' Dewey expanded ' *Library association record 9* 1907 307-322.

19 W C Berwick Sayers made a wry comment on this in his *Manual of classification* 4th edition revised by Arthur Maltby (Deutsch, 1967): ' No doubt in any but an ideal state caoutchouc will oust learning. So small was the interest in the fate of this patiently built up enterprise that *The Times* refused to accept a short letter of protest ' (p 180).

20 The sections published in 1943 comprised a single volume covering Class 0 Generalities and the common auxiliaries, and three volumes covering the whole of science : 5/53 Mathematics, Astronomy, Physics; 54 Chemistry; 55/59 Geology and the Biological sciences. These were originally compiled under the direction of the British Society for International Bibliography in its capacity as British member of FID, but were finally published by the British Standards Institution when it took over this particular activity. The British Society for International Bibliography eventually merged with the Association of Special Libraries and Information Bureaux to become Aslib, which has remained the British member of FID and has also taken a continuing interest in the development of UDC.

These sections, which one might well consider to be those most in need of constant revision, are thus some thirty years old.

21 Cf the articles by G A Lloyd and R Dubuc on the proposed major reallocations of the notation in *Revue internationale de documentation 30* 1963 131-140.

It is interesting to note that the fifth edition of Dewey's scheme already showed considerable imbalance between the various classes, which had started out equal only twenty years previously. The tabulation is as follows:

000	105 headings
100	309
200	540
300	552
400	167
500	1694
600	1350
700	531
800	1530
900	640

Science and technology already account for some 41 percent of the total of 7,418 divisions, rather than the 20 percent allocated to them, but of this 41 percent the largest single item is Medicine, with its 820 divisions forming no less than 11 percent of the complete schedules! Literature is a substantial schedule because at this time Dewey enumerated large numbers of individual authors; thus it occupies slightly more than 20 percent of the schedules overall, a rather different proportion to that which we find in more recent editions, for example the eighteenth, where class 800 represents 651 out of the total of 17,132 headings—rather less than 4 percent, an interesting reflection of the far greater degree of synthesis now to be found in this class.

22 Fédération Internationale de Documentation *UDC revision procedure*. First published 1953 as FID 268; revised as FID 283, 1955; redrafted as FID 338, 1961; latest version, FID 429, 1968. Though the latest edition does mention the word facet, it gives no guidance on how a prospective reviser should recognize the facets in his subject area, nor does it give any help on the allocation of notation, except in a few very brief paragraphs concerned with direct subdivision: do not use 1 or 9 if possible, use centesimal notation if there are more than eight or so concepts to be listed. Most of the manual is still concerned with the mechanics of schedule submission, approval and publication.

23 Dubuc, R *La classification décimale universelle* Gauthier-Villars, second edition 1966 (FID 349) p 70-83.

24 The draft of this schedule was compiled in 1958, and was in use in the library of A V Roe Ltd, later part of Hawker Siddeley Dynamics Ltd, from that time. Published as a P-Note (848) in 1966, it appears in *Extensions and corrections* series 6:2 September 1966.

25 This schedule, compiled by C S Sabel, H Coblans and A C Foskett, was submitted to the International Subject Committee in 1960, published as a P-Note in early 1962 and appeared in *Extensions and corrections* in 1962.

26 Vickery, B C 'The UDC and technical information indexing' *Unesco bulletin 15* 1961 126-138, 147.

Kyle, B 'The Universal Decimal Classification: a study of the present position and future developments, with particular reference to those schedules which deal with the humanities, arts and social sciences' *Unesco bulletin 15* 1961 53-69.

27 Caless, T W and others *Strategies for manipulating Universal Decimal Classification relationships for computer retrieval* (Washington, DC, Biological Sciences Communication Project 1970).

Includes Foskett, A C 'Instructions for UDC schedule revisions' p 23-30.

28 *Universal Decimal Classification: abridged English edition* (British Standards Institution, 1948). (BS1000A: 1948; FID 289.)

29 *Universal Decimal Classification: trilungual abridged edition* (The Hague, FID 1958). (FID 277; BS1000B: 1958.)

Universal Decimal Classification: 10-year supplement to abridged editions (FID/Unesco, 1969). This supplement contains such additions as the Persons auxiliary, –05, and the Author's point-of-view auxiliary, .000.0/.9.

30 Mills, J 'Full, medium and abridged editions of UDC' (*in* ref 27 p 6-12).

CHAPTER 3

31 An index to the computer schedule is now being produced.

32 We may compare this situation with the very similar one which holds for the Library of Congress classification. However, for the latter, the list of *Subject headings . . .*, which gives LC class numbers, does serve as a kind of index, and there are also some cross-references from the index to one set of schedules to particular class numbers in other schedules; *eg* if we look in the index to Religion BL-BX for the class number for Freemasons, we are referred to HS397 in Social sciences H. Neither of these ameliorations is available in UDC, so that concepts which are too detailed to be listed in the abridged editions may be quite difficult to find.

33 This work will be discussed in more detail in chapter 5. At this point, it will be sufficient to mention that obtaining complete,

workable, schedules was perhaps the biggest single problem the project workers had to overcome.

34 *Universal Decimal Classification : Special subject edition for nuclear science and technology* (The Hague, FID 1964). (FID 351).

35 *Universal Decimal Classification : Special subject edition for metallurgy* (Iron and Steel Institute, 1964). (FID 362).

36 The Special subject edition for nuclear science and technology (ref 34) was based on the UKAEA *Code of practice*. However, within the authority, libraries abbreviated 621.039 to N, and also had rules for citation order in certain areas (particularly those where it was thought necessary to reverse colon combinations) which do not form part of the published version.

It is worth noting that the Russians have apparently concentrated on making large numbers of special subject editions available rather than trying to translate the full schedules as a unit. The Americans have in their turn translated *Some principal divisions of Soviet Universal Classification table* from the Russian version of the abridged edition published in 1962! (JPRS: 37,284).

37 Wellisch, H ' New publication methods for the UDC: a proposal ' *Revue internationale de documentation 27* 1960 145-148.

38 Rigby, M *Mechanization of the UDC: final report on pilot project to further explore possibilities for mechanization of UDC schedules* (Washington, DC, American Meteorological Society, 1964). (PB 166 412.)

Rigby, M ' Experiments in mechanized control of meteorological and geoastrophysical literature and the UDC schedules in these fields ' *Revue internationale de documentation 31* 1964 103-106.

39 Ayres, F and others ' Some applications of mechanization in a large special library ' *Journal of documentation 23* 1967 34-44. A computer was used to produce an authority file of UDC numbers actually in use, together with an alphabetical subject index.

40 Linford, J ' Books in English ' *Library Association record 74* 1972 9.

Larkworthy, G and Brown, C G ' Library catalogues on microfilm ' *Library Association record 73* 1971 231-232.

41 Foskett, A C ' Misogynists all: a study in critical classification ' *Library resources and technical services 15* 1971 117-121.

42 These broad subject groupings prepared by the Committee on Scientific and Technical Information of the US Federal Council for Science and Technology are most easily available, though in slightly

modified form, in the EJC *Thesaurus of engineering and scientific terms* (New York, Engineers Joint Council, 1967). (Usually known as TEST.)

43 Foskett, A C *The subject approach to information* (ref 13) p 103.

44 One should not overlook here the pressure arising from the use of DC numbers on Library of Congress cards. Many libraries use these cards as cataloguing copy, and are therefore under some obligation to conform to the classification schedules used, *ie* the current edition.

45 The work of Marshall McLuhan is not irrelevant here in its suggestion that we tend to take the vehicle of a message as the message itself.

46 McCrosky, J 'Is classification dead?' [letter to the editor] *Library journal* February 15 1969 695.

47 Foskett, A C 'Shelf classification—*or else*' *Library journal* September 1 1970 2771-2773. A very detailed study of the role of shelf classification has been carried out by R J Hyman *Access to library collections: an inquiry into the validity of the direct shelf approach, with special reference to browsing* (Scarecrow Press, 1972). His conclusions seem to reinforce the view that to use shelf classification purely as a locating device is a 'waste of rich potential'.

48 Foskett, A C *The subject approach to information* (ref 13) p 96.

49 The first edition of the English Electric Company's *Classification of engineering* put the primary facet, Machines, first in the schedules, ignoring the principle of inversion. The preface to the second and third editions contains an acknowledgement that this was later felt to be a mistake, because it did not lead to a situation where general always preceded special.

50 Caless, T W and Kirk, D B 'An application of UDC to machine searching' *Journal of documentation* 23 1967 208-215.

51 Perreault, J M 'Order of operations and use of square brackets' (*in* ref 27 p 18-21).

Perreault, J M *Towards a theory for UDC* (Bingley, 1969). See chapter V 'Towards explication of the rules of formation in UDC' p 59-85.

52 Wellisch, H *Bonds and bonding of UDC notational symbols.* Letter to G A Lloyd and members of FID/CCC December 15 1969 4p.

53 P-Note 947, included in *Extensions and corrections* series 7, covers the use of square brackets and the double colon.

54 Perreault, J M *Towards a theory for UDC* (Bingley, 1969). See chapters VIII 'Categories and relators: a new schema' and IX 'Emendations to the relator-schema' p 119-148. The schema was circulated as P-Note 958 in 1968, and drew a quantity of criticism, most of it

unfavourable. It seems unlikely that it will ever become a successful part of UDC, though it represents a response to a very real need—the clarification of the role of the colon; this is also discussed in Kervégant, P ' Classification et analyse de relations ' *Bulletin des bibliothèques de France* 4 1959 495-511.

55 Van Nostrand's *Scientific encyclopedia* (4th edition, 1968).

56 Lancaster, F W ' On the need for role indicators in postcoordinate retrieval systems ' *American documentation* 19 1968 42-46.

57 Keen, E M and Digger, J *Report on an information science index languages test* (College of Librarianship Wales, 1972).

58 *UNISIST: Study report on the feasibility of a world science information system* (Paris, Unesco, 1971). An abbreviated version is available as a *Synopsis* of the above, also published by Unesco in 1971.

59 Ziman, J M *Public knowledge: the social dimension of science* (Cambridge University Press, 1968).

60 Terry, J E Private communication. Although a great deal of work has been done on international cooperation in the field of nuclear science and technology, little has been published. In an article entitled ' Nuclear science abstracts: a twenty-year perspective ' R L Shannon mentions in passing that ' The successful publication of NSA . . . is also the result of goodwill substantially enriched by international support ', though the abstract of his paper promises a discussion of decentralized input to NSA. (*Symposium on the handling of nuclear information* International Atomic Energy Agency 1970 p 379-384.) INIS, the Intenational Nuclear Information Service, is a further example of this essential cooperation.

61 Vickery, B C and others *Classification in science information: a comparative study undertaken by Aslib for the International Council of Scientific Unions* (Aslib, 1969). (UNISIST/CSI/5.8)

62 Schmidt, A F *Reform of the UDC* (FID, 1971). (FID C71-21) [Translation circulated to members of BSI Committee OC/20/4 by BSI as 71/80498].

62a Schmidt, A F ' Gedanken zur Reform der Dezimalklassifikation ' *Nachrichten für Dokumentation* 23 1972 105-113.

63 Dahlberg, I ' Possibilities for a new Universal Decimal Classification ' *Journal of documentation* 27 1971 18-36. Originally published in German in *Nachrichten für Dokumentation* 21 1970 143-151; a revised version has been published in the 1971 FID Symposium (ref 94c below).

64 Weizäcker, C F von 'Die Zukunft der Wissenschaft' *Die Zeit* (50) 1969 51-53 (quoted in ref 63).

65 In the Library of Loughborough Technical College, this separation meant at one point that books on some aspects of Engineering were separated from those on other aspects by a single bay of books on Social sciences, of which the library at that time had but few. The overall effect was somewhat odd, and many of the users must have found it unhelpful. Bliss devoted most of his life to a study of main class order, without however achieving a result so superior that it has been universally accepted. [cf Foskett, A C *The subject approach to information* (ref 13) p 114 *et seq.*]

66 Seminal mnemonics are discussed in Ranganathan's *Prolegomena* (ref 10) and in *Colon classification;* see Foskett, A C *The subject approach to information* (ref 13) for the view held by the present author that they represent a case of notation dictating order.

67 Bentham, G and Hooker, Sir J D *Genera plantarum* revised edition by J D Hutchinson (Clarendon Press, 1964-). To be complete in twelve volumes.

68 British National Bibliography. *Supplementary classification schedules* (BNB, 1963). The common subdivisions identified by BNB include, among others, Statistics, Persons, Organizations, Information and Research, with their subdivisions.

69 A 'phoenix' schedule is one which completely replaces an earlier version, using the same notation. So far, DC has revised Psychology, Mathematics, Law and parts of Chemistry in this way.

70 Lloyd, G A 'The Universal Decimal Classification as an international switching language' (*in Subject retrieval in the seventies: proceedings of an international symposium... 1971*. Bingley; University of Maryland, School of Library and Information Services, 1972 p 116-125).

71 Coates, E J 'Switching languages for indexing' *Journal of documentation 26* 1970 102-110.

72 Terry, J E Private communication. The results of the study made at AERE, Harwell, were not published, but they showed a rapid fall in the use made of the old catalogue to a low but not zero level. Some use is still made of it, in fact, but this is small in comparison with use of the current catalogue.

73 Wellisch, H 'Organisatorische Neuordnung des DK-Systems' *Nachrichten für Dokumentation 22* 1971 55-63. [*Translation circulated to members of BSI Committee OC/20/4 by BSI as 71/80497.*]

74 FID/CCC Document C71-18 (private circulation).

75 It would seem that recent proposals for the revision of the schedules for Electrical engineering 621.3 have been put on one side pending a decision about the introduction of the SRC. Schmidt himself writes (ref 62a) that:

'he accepted the chairmanship of the UDC revision committee for the electrical engineering section only on the condition that before the continuation of the revision work in this field the FID/CCC would at last come to a final decision on a series of questions, that clear rules for the practical revision work were laid down and their general application safeguarded by a general revision . . .'

CHAPTER 5

76 Ashthorpe, H D 'The punched-card indexing experiment at the library of the Atomic Energy Research Establishment, Harwell' *Aslib proceedings 4* 1952 101-104.

77 Lancaster, F W 'Interaction between requesters and a large mechanized retrieval system' *Information storage and retrieval 4* 1968 239-252.

78 See Foskett, A C *The subject approach to information* (ref 13) p 176 for a demonstration of the use of verbal extensions.

79 Mentioned by Lloyd in ref 70, this gesture towards mechanization is a step in the right direction, but one can hardly regard it as anything but another example of the inadequate reaction of FID to the urgent needs of the situation.

80 Rigby, M 'The UDC in mechanized information retrieval' (*in Subject retrieval in the seventies,* quoted in ref 70 p 126-142).

81 Freeman, R R *Research project for the evaluation of the UDC as the indexing language for a mechanized reference retrieval system: an introduction* (American Institute of Physics, 1965). (AIP/DRP UDC-1.)

Freeman, R R *Research project for the evaluation of the UDC as the indexing language for a mechanized reference retrieval system: progress report for the period July 1, 1965-January 21, 1966* (American Institute of Physics, 1966). (AIP/DRP UDC-2.)

Freeman, R R *Modern approaches to the management of a classification* (American Institute of Physics, 1966). (AIP/UDC-3.) Also published as 'The management of a classification . . .' quoted as ref 16.

Russell, M and Freeman, R R *Computer-aided indexing of a scientific abstracts journal by the UDC with UNIDEK: a case study* (American Institute of Physics, 1967). (AIP/UDC-4).

Freeman, R R and Atherton, P *File organization and search strategy using the Universal Decimal Classification in mechanized reference retrieval systems* (American Institute of Physics, 1967). (AIP/UDC-5.) Also published in Samuelson, K *Mechanized information storage, retrieval and dissemination: proceedings of the FID/IFIP Joint Conference, Rome, June 14-17, 1967* (North-Holland Publishing Company, 1968 p 122-152).

Freeman, R R *Evaluation of the retrieval of metallurgical document references using the Universal Decimal Classification in a computer-based system* (American Institute of Physics, 1968). (AIP/UDC-6.)

Freeman, R R and Atherton, P *AUDACIOUS—an experiment with an on-line, interactive reference retrieval system using the Universal Decimal Classification as the index language in the field of nuclear science* (American Institute of Physics, 1968). (AIP/UDC-7.)

Atherton, P, King, D W and Freeman, R R *Evaluation of the retrieval of nuclear science document references using the Universal Decimal Classification in a computer-based system* (American Institute of Physics, 1968). (AIP/UDC-8.)

Freeman, R R and Atherton, P *Final report of the research project for the evaluation of the UDC as the indexing language for a mechanized reference retrieval system* (American Institute of Physics, 1968). (AIP/UDC-9.) Also published in the *Proceedings of the first seminar on UDC in a mechanized retrieval system* ref 94a below. Reports AIP/UDC-3, AIP/UDC-7 and AIP/UDC-9 may be singled out as the key documents produced by this important project.

82 Freeman, R R ' Computers and classification systems ' *Journal of documentation 20* 1964 137-145.

83 Freeman, R R *Summary of the status of the Universal Decimal Classification in English, including progress by the AIP/UDC Project through June 1, 1967* (American Institute of Physics, 1967). (AIP/UDC Project Newsletter No 3.)

This newsletter also includes a page showing results of computer-controlled typesetting, included in the text as figure 1, and a list of the data bases for retrieval experimentation. This was distributed by Freeman and Atherton at a meeting organized by Aslib on June 9 1967, to hear a report on their progress with the AIP/UDC Project. A note circulated at a meeting of the US National Committee in March 1969 points out that the master file created by merging all available English UDC schedules is available in microfiche form from the ERIC Document Reproduction Service as ED-019-980 (containing 3069 pages) while the 'medium' edition for classes 0/3, 5 and 7/9 is available from the same source as ED-019-979 (689 pages).

84 It would appear that the total cost of the full English edition is likely to exceed £70 per copy, and may well be higher still if printing costs continue to rise. The abridged edition costs £3, but a revised edition of this would be a great deal more expensive. For comparison, the current edition of DC costs approximately £18. The costs for COM quoted by Larkworthy and Brown (ref 40) for a 1,000 page catalogue were £50 for the master film and £313 for twenty copies, about £18 per copy. To this must be added the cost of a reader, but as more and more material becomes available in this form, libraries are likely to have this equipment as a matter of course. There is the further point that COM costs are likely to decrease as conventional printing costs rise.

85 Freeman, R R 'The management of a classification . . .' (ref 16).

86 FID Congress, Washington DC 1965. *Proceedings* (FID, 1966).

87 Prentice, D D and others *1401 Information storage and retrieval system: the Combined File Search System* (IBM 1401 General Program Library No 1401-10.3.047)version 2). San Jose, California IBM 1965).

88 AIP/UDC-5, quoted in ref 81.

89 The role of human error in information retrieval failure was first firmly established by the Cranfield Project. For a consideration of this question see A C Foskett *The subject approach to information* (ref 13) p 20 and p 365 *et seq*. Searches involving NOT logic do not lend themselves particularly well to manual techniques; normally one would need to ignore the NOT command, carry out the search and then remove those items which fell into the proscribed category. Searches involving a stem and a suffix which may or may not be joined directly to the stem (*eg* 621.384.6xxx15) can be conducted in a manual system if the alphabetical index is complete and properly compiled; to conduct such a search through the classified file alone could be extremely tedious and result in a high error level.

90 The first largescale publication to deal with this problem was *Computer filing of index, bibliographic and catalog entries*, by T C Hines and J C Harris (Newark, Brodart, 1966). There is also a British standard, *Alphabetical arrangement and the filing of numerals and symbols* (BS1749: 1969). The Library Association Cataloguing and Indexing Group convened a Working Party which has produced a report under the chairmanship of J W Jolliffe. A substantial report has been produced by the Library of Congress, and further work on the comparison of these two reports has been carried out by R M Duchesne of BNB and

Mrs G Walker of the College of Librarianship Wales. The only firm conclusion that one can reach at the present time is that no general agreement has been reached, and that a great deal of work remains to be done before complete international agreement is feasible. In the meantime, we may be producing large quantities of machine-readable records which do not contain enough information to permit us to sort them into an acceptable filing order, bearing in mind that not all computers follow the same set of rules.

91 See Foskett, A C *The subject approach to information* (ref 13) p 148 *et seq* for a discussion of flexibility in notation.

92 AIP/UDC-7, quoted in ref 81.

93 As a member of the British committee since 1965, the present author must take his share of any blame that may arise from what now appears to be an error of judgement. At the time, it seemed best to press on with the work on the full edition.

One use of the AIP/UDC magnetic tapes is reported in the Herceg Novi Symposium (ref 94c). This is in the paper 'The study of UDC and other indexing languages through computer manipulation of machine-readable data bases' by G A Cooke, D M Heaps and M Mercier. This suggests the use of UDC in concordance with a thesaurus for indexing water resources material, and demonstrates the feasibility of this.

94a Seminar on UDC in a mechanized retrieval system; conducted by R R Freeman and Pauline Atherton, Copenhagen, 2nd-6th September 1968. *Proceedings;* edited by R Mölgaard-Hansen and Malcolm Rigby (Danish Centre for Documentation, 1969). (FID/CR Report no 9.)

94b Seminar on UDC and mechanized information systems; conducted by Robert R Freeman, Frankfurt, 1st-5th June 1970. *Proceedings;* edited by R Mölgaard-Hansen and Margit Westring-Nielsen (Danish Centre for Documentation, 1971). (FID/CR Report no 11.)

94c International symposium: UDC in relation to other index languages, held in Herceg Novi, Yugoslavia, June 28-July 1, 1971. *Proceedings* (Yugoslav Center for Technical and Scientific Documentation, 1972).

95 Caless, T W 'Subject analysis matrices for classification with UDC' (*in* ref 94a).

96 Cutler, E M and Caless, T W *The feasibility of automated search on pre-coordinated classification systems.* Paper presented to the US National Committee, December 4 1969. (Private circulation.)

97 Webber, J 'Die *Documentatio geographica* . . . eine Beispiel für die Anwendung der DK in der Geographie' (*in* ref 94b p 21-41).

Koch, K-H ' Maschinelle Herstellung der *Documentatio geographica* unter besonderer Berücksichtigung der DK ' (*in* ref 94b p 43-45).

98 Ayres, F H, Cayless, C F and German, J A ' Some applications of mechanization in a lrage special library ' *Journal of documentation 23* 1967 34-44.

Corbett, L ' The use of UDC and computer-aided literature processing at UKAEA, Aldermaston ' (*in* ref 94b p 142-147).

99 McCash, W H and Carmichael, J J: ' UDC user profiles as developed for a computer-based SDI service in the Iron and Steel industry ' *Journal of documentation 26* 1970 295-312.

CHAPTER 6

100 Foskett, D J ' The Classification Research Group, 1952-1962 ' *Libri 12* 1962 127-138.

Crossley, C A ' New schemes of classification: principles and practice ' *Library Association record 65* 1963 51-59.

Wilson, T D ' The work of the British Classification Research Group ' (*in Subject retrieval in the seventies,* quoted in ref 70 p 62-71). For a comprehensive list of CRG Bulletins see Foskett, A C *The subject approach to information* (ref 13) p 381.

101 Courses in ' the construction and maintenance of index languages ' form part of the syllabuses at the University of Maryland School of Library and Information Services and at the College of Librarianship Wales, and no doubt at other library schools; certainly at the two institutions with which the author is familiar no difficulty has been found in getting students to compile model classification schemes on a wide variety of topics from Psychiatry to Agriculture and Cookery.

102 Library Association *Some problems of a general classification scheme: report of a conference held in London, June 1963* (Library Association, 1964).

103 Classification Research Group: *Classification and information control* (Library Association, 1969). (Library Association Research Publications no 1.)

103a Austin, D W *Fields, categories and general systems theory: (Naturally occurring entities)* Report to the Classification Research Group 1968. (Unpublished.)

104 Foskett, D J ' Classification and integrative levels ' *in The Sayers memorial volume;* edited by B I Palmer and D J Foskett (Library Assocation, 1960).

105 The term 'mentefact' was coined by Barbara Kyle, one of the members of the CRG, to refer to mental constructs in the same way that 'artefact' refers to physical constructs.

106 Harte, Bret 'Plain language from Truthful James' 1870.

107 Feibleman, J 'Integrative levels in nature' *in* Kyle, B *Focus on information and communication* (Aslib, 1968 p 27-41).

108 Quoted by Austin (ref 103) without attribution.

109 McMillan, O and Gonzalez, R F *Systems analysis: a computer approach to decision models* (Irwin, 1968).

110 This rule goes at least as far back as W S Merrill's *Code for classifiers* (American Library Association, 1928); though, as one might expect, Merrill does not give one single rule but eight, to cover particular cases.

111a Foskett, A C *The subject approach to information* (ref 13) p 67-74.

111b Austin, D W Private communication. The new set of operators is to be published in the *PRECIS: Manual of indexing,* to be published by BNB (1973?).

112 Aitchison, J, Gomersall, A and Ireland, R *Thesaurofacet: a thesaurus and faceted classification for engineering and related subjects* (Whetstone, English Electric Company Ltd, 1970).

Aitchison, J 'Thesaurofacet: a multipurpose retrieval language tool' *Journal of documentation* 26 1970 187-203.

Aitchison, J 'Thesaurofacet: a new concept in subject retrieval schemes' *in Subject retrieval in the seventies,* quoted in ref 70 p 72-98.

113 Roget, Peter Mark *Thesaurus of English words and phrases.* First published 1852, and now available in a variety of editions.

114 It is clear that the term 'list of subject headings' is reserved by 'information specialists', particularly in the United States, for lists such as that of Sears or the Library of Congress. These have been found inadequate for technical information retrieval, and the term has therefore acquired a somewhat pejorative connotation. However, a study of such tools as the ERIC *Thesaurus* shows that the headings are indistinguishable in their construction from those in the so-called subject headings lists; the only improvement lies perhaps in the more precise designation of relationships one usually finds in a thesaurus. For examples, see A C Foskett *The subject approach to information* (ref 13) p 317 *et seq.*

115 Problems arising from synthesis of notation are discussed in A C Foskett *The subject approach to information* (ref 137) p 134 and p 144 *et seq*. Ranganathan has claimed that CC gives on average shorter notation than does DC for the same composite subject; a similar result may well hold good for UDC, where lengthy notation is almost the rule.

116 A very detailed bibliography on *The acceptibility of notation* was compiled by L V Quiney as part requirement for the University of London Diploma in Librarianship, 1966.

CHAPTER 7

117 Maltby, A *Classification in the 1970's* (Bingley, 1972). This contains chapters on the five major schemes and on various other aspects of classification theory and development; all of these would agree that ' we are not interested in the possibilities of defeat '.

118 Lloyd, G A ' The UDC in its international aspects ' *Aslib proceedings 21* 1969, 204-208. In this paper, Lloyd reports the result of an FID survey aimed at finding out the distribution of UDC editions throughout the world. From the returns for a dozen centres, including four of the major users, it appears that the total number of copies of all published sections of full editions exceeds 100,000; the actual number of full editions sold (*ie* as complete sets) is rather less than a fifth of this figure; abridged editions, 50,000; special subject editions, guides etc, 20,000. These very satisfactory figures must however be compared with the circulation of about 300 for P-Notes reported in C72-24 (ref 136), which suggests that by no means all of the *purchasers* can be current *users*.

119 Schedules for the depth classification version of CC have been appearing in *Annals of library science* and *Library science with a slant to documentation* at intervals for some years now, but the subject areas covered so far have been relatively few and rather specialized.

120 Foskett, A C ' The subject approach: recent developments in indexing ' *Journal of librarianship 4* 1972 240-252.

121 This point was made very forcibly by R C Griffin, Librarian of the Chemical Society, at the meeting on July 6 1972 (ref 140) and at meetings of the British National Committee. Chemistry is also mentioned by Lloyd (ref 118) as being one of those areas where revision has been too slow.

122 Schon, D *Towards the stable state* (BBC Reith Lectures, 1970). The main thesis of these lectures was the conflict between our desire for change and our need for stability in the environment. In the past,

the pace of change has been tolerable, but with the development of technology changes are now taking place at a faster rate than society as a whole finds comfortable.

123 The bibliographical services of the British Library formed the theme of the 1972 Annual Conference of the Library Association Cataloguing and Indexing Group.

124 Lloyd, G A : quoted from a letter to the author.

125 Foskett, A C *The subject approach to information* (ref 13) p 105.

126 FID/CCC C72-21 *Progress with the SRC Project*. (Limited circulation.)

127 Schmidt, A F and de Wijn, J H *Some possibilities for a new ' reformed ' UDC* (FID, 1972). (Limited circulation.)

128 Davison, K *Classification practice in Britain: report on a survey of classification opinion and practice in Great Britain, with particular reference to the Dewey Decimal Classification* (Library Association, 1966). Of 474 libraries reported as using DDC, 8 were using editions earlier than the 14th, 5 were using the 14th on its own, 124 14th+16th, 23 14th+15th+16th, and 16 13th+14th+16th. Since this survey, the 17th and 18th editions have appeared, and a similar enquiry now would probably reveal a more up-to-date picture overall.

129 Aitchison, J 'Practical application of facet classification with special reference to the English Electric faceted classification for engineering ' *in* Bakewell, K G B *Classification for information retrieval* (Bingley, 1968 p 43-72).

130 Soergel, D 'A general model for indexing languages: the basis for compatibility and integration ' *in Subject retrieval in the seventies*, quoted in ref 70 p 36-61). Soergel emphasizes the important distinction to be made between subject analysis, which is not restricted, and file organization, which usually is.

131 Schmidt, A F (ref 62a).

132 This is most clearly stated in the introduction to the EJC *Thesaurus* published in 1964; selection of descriptors seems to have involved more extensive editorial effort in the *Thesaurus of engineering and scientific terms*, but it is fairly clear that a term found only in one of the lists examined was unlikely to be included.

133 Wellisch, H ' Subject retrieval in the seventies—methods, problems, prospects ' (*in Subject retrieval in the seventies*, quoted in ref 70 p 2-27).

134 Foskett, A C *The subject approach to information* (ref 13) p 86 *et seq*. The point is discussed in most standard texts.

135 See, for example, the chapters on 'user studies' in *Annual review of information science and technology,* edited by C Cuadra.

136 FID/CCC C72-24. *Proposed arrangements and publication procedures for P-Notes, current 'Extensions' and (future) UDC supplements* 1972. (Private circulation.)

137 Dewey, M *Dewey decimal classification and relative index* 18th edition p 3-5.

138 The exact figure given (ref 137 p 69) is 37,139 copies.

CHAPTER 8

139 Eaton, T 'Epitaph to a dead classification' *Library association record* 57 1955 428-430.

140 The complete paper read by G A Lloyd, and summaries of the other papers presented, are given in *Aslib proceedings* 24 October 1972. A more detailed version of his paper ' SRC: unverified assumptions ' was circulated by D Newcombe before the meeeting.

141 Roberts, N 'Desiderata for national bibliographical services' *Aslib proceedings* 24 1972 473-479

142 Weeks, D, Benton, M and Thomas, M L *Universal Decimal Classification: a selected bibliography of UDC literature* (Washington DC, Biological Sciences Communication Project, 1971). 384 references, up to 1970, arranged in one sequence alphabetically by author.

APPENDIX A

143 Arntz, H ' Die DK—eine Vielfacettenklassifikation ' *Nachrichten für Dokumentation* 21 1970 139-142.

144 Ohman, E and Olivecrona, C ' Some notational, hierarchic and syntactic problems in connection with concordances between UDC and thesauri ' (*in* ref 94c).

145 MeSH (ref 7) is used in the compilation of *Index medicus* and the MEDLARS system, and is revised continuously for this purpose; it is therefore not surprising that it is more satisfactory than the corresponding UDC schedules, which are now several years old, though the English translation has only appeared relatively recently.

146 Stueart, R D 'An analysis of the Universal Decimal Classification as a term system for Nuclear science and technology ' *Library resources and technical services* 15 1971 339-411.

147 Ohman, E ' H Arntz's criticism of UDC in the light of investigations on concordances between the UDC and thesauri ' *Nachrichten für Dokumentation* 23 1972 65-68.

148 EURATOM *Thesaurus* 1964. For a description, see (for example) Colbach, R ' Thesaurus structure and generic posting' *in Handling of nuclear information: proceedings of a symposium . . . 1970* (International Atomic Energy Agency, 1970 p 585-592).

149 Wellisch H 'A concordance between UDC and Thesaurus of engineering and scientific terms (TEST). Results of a pilot project' (*in* ref 94c). Unfortunately, no funds have been forthcoming to continue this valuable study.

INDEX

References in roman type are to page numbers; references in italic type are to items in the Bibliography and notes. As the whole work deals with UDC there are no index entries at this heading.